BRITISH AND IRISH

Introductory critical

SAMUEL BEC

While providing a critical introduction for the student of Samuel Beckett's work, and for other readers and theatre-goers who have been influenced by it, this study also presents an original perspective on one of the century's greatest writers of prose fiction and drama. Andrew Kennedy links Beckett's vision of a diminished humanity with his art of formally and verbally diminished resources, and traces the fundamental simplicity – and coherence – of Beckett's work beneath its complex textures. In a section on the plays, Dr Kennedy stresses the humour and tragicomic humanism alongside the theatrical effectiveness; and in a discussion of the fiction (the celebrated trilogy of novels) he relates the relentless diminution of the 'story' to the diminishing selfhood of the narrator. An introduction outlines the personal, cultural and specifically literary contexts of Beckett's writing, while a concluding chapter offers up-to-date reflections on his *œuvre*, from the point of view of the themes highlighted throughout the book.

This study, complete with a chronological table and a guide to further reading, will prove stimulating for both beginners and advanced students of Beckett.

BRITISH AND IRISH AUTHORS
Introductory critical studies

In the same series:

SAMUEL BECKETT

ANDREW K. KENNEDY

Department of English
University of Bergen

CAMBRIDGE UNIVERSITY PRESS

CAMBRIDGE

NEW YORK   PORT CHESTER

MELBOURNE   SYDNEY

Published by Press Syndicate of the University of Cambridge
The Pitt Building, Trumpington Street, Cambridge CB2 1RP
40 West 20th Street, New York, NY 10011-4211, USA
10 Stamford Road, Oakleigh, Melbourne 3166, Australia

First published 1989
Reprinted 1991

Printed in Great Britain at
the University Press, Cambridge

British Library cataloguing in publication data

Kennedy, Andrew K. (Andrew Karpati), *1931–*
Samuel Beckett
1. English literature, Beckett, Samuel,
1906 – Critical Studies
I. Title   II. Series
828′.91209

Library of Congress cataloguing in publication data applied for

ISBN 0 521 25482 5 hardback
ISBN 0 521 27488 5 paperback

GG

For Ruby Cohn

Contents

CONTENTS

Acknowledgements

I wish to thank the Norwegian Research Council for Science and the Humanities for a grant that enabled me to complete this study at Clare Hall, Cambridge – that ideal working place – in the spring and summer of 1987.

Chronology

The following is a selective chronology of Beckett's life with the dates of publication or first performance of principal works. For fuller details of the works discussed at length in this book, see the Select bibliography on p. 166.

1906   Born at Foxrock, near Dublin, allegedly on Good Friday, 13 April

1920–3 Portora Royal School, Ulster

1923–7 Trinity College, Dublin. Read Modern languages (English, French and Italian)

1927–8 Taught for two terms at Campbell College, Belfast

1928   Began two-year exchange fellowship at l'Ecole Normale Supérieure as *Lecteur d'anglais*. Met Joyce

1929   Published short story 'Assumption' in *transition*, 16–17; and first criticism, 'Dante . . . Bruno. Vico . . . Joyce', in *Our Exagmination*

1930   Published *Whoroscope* (poem on Descartes), which won a £10 prize from Hours Press

1931   Published *Proust* in London (criticism). MA Trinity College, Dublin, and resigned from post of Assistant in French there

1932   After six months in Kassel began a period of wanderings in Germany, France, England and Ireland. Began *Dream of Fair to Middling Women*, which draws on these journeys

1933   Father died, leaving Beckett a £200 annuity. Lived for about two years in Chelsea, London, supplementing his annuity by reviewing and translation

1934   Published *More Pricks than Kicks* (short stories). Began analysis at Tavistock Clinic

1935   Published *Echo's Bones* (collection of thirteen poems)

1937   Settled in Paris

1938   Published *Murphy* in London (a novel in English,

begun in 1934 – rejected by forty-two publishers before acceptance by Routledge)

Stabbed in a Paris street, 7 January. Visited in hospital by pianist Suzanne Dumesnil, who later became his wife

1939   Returned to Paris, from a visit to Dublin, at the outbreak of the Second World War

1941–2   Worked in the French Resistance with his friend Alfred Péron

1942   The Gestapo arrested Péron; Beckett and Suzanne Dumesnil fled from Paris to Roussillon in unoccupied France. Began writing *Watt*

1945   Worked for Irish Red Cross in Normandy. Received *Croix de Guerre* and *Médaille de la Résistance* for his service in war-time France. Visited Ireland, and finished *Watt* in Dublin

1946   Began his most creative period, writing in French, with *Mercier et Camier* (novel) and *Nouvelles* ('La Fin', 'L'Expulsé', 'Le Calmant' and 'Premier Amour' – stories)

1947   Completed *Molloy* and *Eleuthéria* (unpublished play)

1948   Completed *Malone Meurt*

1949   Completed *En attendant Godot* – in January Published *Three Dialogues with Georges Duthuit* in *transition*

1950   Completed *L'Innommable*. The trilogy of novels was accepted for publication by Editions de Minuit in November.
Beckett returned to Dublin before his mother's death in August

1952   *En attendant Godot* published in Paris

1953   *En attendant Godot* first performed at the Théâtre de Babylone, Paris.

1955   *Waiting for Godot* produced in London. Began *Fin de Partie* (*Endgame*)

1956   *Waiting for Godot* published in London

1957   *All that Fall* broadcast by BBC Third Programme. World première of *Fin de Partie* (in French) in London

1958   World première of *Krapp's Last Tape* in London

1961 World première of *Happy Days* in New York.
      Comment c'est (*How It Is*) published in Paris

1963 World première of *Play* (in German) in Ulm

1969 Awarded the Nobel Prize for Literature, 23 October.
      Accepted the award but did not attend the prize-
      giving ceremony in Stockholm

1970 *Lessness* published in London

1972 World première of *Not I* in New York

1976 *That Time* and *Footfalls* première at the Royal Court
      Theatre to celebrate Beckett's seventieth birthday

1977 *Ghost Trio* and . . . *but the clouds* broadcast on BBC
      Television

1981 *Ill Seen Ill Said* published in *New Yorker*. World
      première of *Rockaby* and *Ohio Impromptu* in Buffalo and
      at Ohio State Beckett Symposium respectively

1982 World première of *Catastrophe* at Avignon Festival

1984 *Collected Shorter Plays of Samuel Beckett* published in
      London

1986 Beckett's eightieth birthday celebrated with con-
      ferences in Paris, New York, and Stirling, unattended
      by Beckett

Note on texts

References to Beckett's texts are to the following single-title editions:

Waiting for Godot, Faber, London, Second edition 1965, reprinted 1981
Endgame, Faber, London, 1958
Krapp's Last Tape, Faber, London, 1959
Happy Days, Faber, London, 1963
Play, Faber, London, 1964

Murphy, Calder, London, 'Jupiter Book', 1963
Molloy, Calder, London, 'Jupiter Book', 1966
Malone Dies, Calder, London, 1975 (new edition of Calder text first published in 1958)
The Unnamable, Calder, London, 1975 (new edition of Calder text first published in 1958)

Introduction

Beckett at eighty plus is eminently visible – a face and a name appropriated by the world – as the leading non-realist Western writer of the second half of our century. This visibility is itself ironic, for he had chosen reclusive privacy in living, and the isolation of the self as an obsessive subject. The narrators of his fiction and the protagonists of most of his plays are incurable soliloquisers. The most memorable image in his only film is a man (played by Buster Keaton) for ever in retreat from a potential observer. The writings of his youth and early manhood were mostly neglected in the thirties and forties and are, with the exception of *Murphy*, not widely read today. Again, the ageing writer of the seventies has produced perfect yet highly compressed 'minimalist' texts which are not likely to become familiar, in the literal as well as in the literary sense – preserving their strangeness beyond reading and performance.

The fame of *Waiting for Godot* (written in 1948 but first performed only in 1953 in Paris and 1955 in London) began to transform Beckett's situation – from the obscure avant-garde writer to the world figure. That particular play, performed everywhere from the San Quentin penitentiary to colleges of education, had become a set book in secondary schools and a relative best-seller by the 1970s. Gradually the more elusive plays and novels also came to attract world-wide attention and – a significant fact for new readers and their guide – a vast array of criticism, comparable only to the industry devoted to major writers of the past. The new situation has brought with it the risk of over-interpretation: it is possible that in Beckett criticism 'more is less', while the inner law of Beckett's work is 'less is more'.

The essential contours of the Beckett terrain will be traced here, not through highly specialised standpoints, but through a sharp focus on the map of contexts leading to an exploration of the ground, the individual works. We find then an overall unity: a vision of diminishing human faculties (a tragicomic failing and falling) written into texts of diminishing language, ever more daringly lessened forms of drama and fiction.

1

It now requires an imaginative effort to reconstruct the original contexts of Beckett's writing – which often cannot be read unaided out of the text of this or that play or novel. The roots of Beckett's art (both the vision of the world and the avant-garde poetics) stretch back to a now almost vanished era: the great fertile phase of modernism in the twenties, accelerated by the First World War. The modernist heritage embraces: a total commitment to writing as an art (which in Beckett is later accompanied by a total scepticism about the possibilities of communication and expression), and the imperative of 'making it new' so that each new work is a venture into the unknown. The central importance of language in all modernist writing becomes, in Beckett, a dangerous immersion in language as a creative/destructive element, language as the stuff that makes up, or else annihilates, the world and the self. (This is the polar opposite of the belief that language comes to us more or less ready-made to represent the world.) Even Beckett's all-encompassing pessimism and spiritual despair – religious symbols used without a structure of belief, the pervasive mysticism of 'nothingness' – spring from a sensibility nearer to the age of Joyce, early Eliot and Kafka, than to the moods and modes of writing dominant now.

The feeling *for* Beckett as a *contemporary* writer is understandable and even helpful in so far as his long creative work – and his impact – stretch into the present. But there is in this seeming contemporaneity also an element of delayed reaction or telescoping: creative maturity reached relatively late in works published with delay (from the mid-fifties on in Britain and America) and then absorbed slowly, in a series of delayed responses, by the wider reading/theatre-going public. Even today public appreciation of Beckett is often superficial or uncomprehending; at the same time, some of his admirers have been tempted to turn him into a cult figure. (In this study evaluation will be mostly implicit, working towards conclusions.) Meanwhile, over three decades Beckett's work has 'kept up with the age', as can be seen, in one conspicuous aspect, in the artistic transformation of several new communicative tools and media: the tape recorder (in *Krapp's Last Tape*), radio (in *All that Fall* and other plays), film and television (the close-up and the voice-over, in *Eh Joe* and in the late plays – *That Time* and *Rockaby*). He has worked closely with a number of gifted actors in three countries (including Billie Whitelaw and Patrick Magee in Britain) and, despite his reclusiveness, he keeps responding promptly to an endless succession of scholarly enquirers. For

a seemingly apolitical writer, Beckett has also shown compassionate awareness of contemporary political conditions: *Catastrophe*
(1982) is dedicated to the persecuted Czech playwright Vaclav
Havel, and the short play dramatises oppression. (In war-time
France, Beckett, a citizen of neutral Ireland, worked for the
Resistance.) Nevertheless in Beckett's work we are entering types
of vision and form no longer of our time, though much in the
achieved work is likely to remain challenging for all time.

Biography, always only partially and controversially relevant to
the study of a writer's work, is particularly problematic as a context for Beckett's work. For Beckett has always endeavoured to
distance and transform the autobiographical elements which are,
without doubt, a main source of his creative work. At times the
author behind the narrator/protagonist becomes visible or audible
– the erudite London-based Murphy, the vision 'at the end of the
jetty' replayed on Krapp's tape, and, in the late work, the voices
returning to the 'old scenes' of Dublin bay in *That Time*.[1] The
biographical context will here be highlighted where it is most
relevant – especially in the nurturing literary environments of
Ireland and Paris – but not given as a self-contained or primary
history.

Similarly, the philosophical context – that is to say, the 'raw
ideas' from Descartes to Sartre that Beckett undoubtedly gathered
and cooked – is to be seen less as a set of intrinsically fruitful
ideas and more as the material of fiction-engendering speculations. Beckett imaginatively incorporates everything at hand –
transmuting a vast array of concepts and conceits from his reading
and professional scholarship (Dante to Proust). Religious ideas are
used as fragments in a creative writer's mythology: with in-
eradicable traces of a Christian education ('We were brought up
like Quakers')[2] leading to a life-long quest for essential meaning,
not to be found. Every work has a religious or metaphysical
dimension, from the subtle 'negative way' of the exploring self in
the trilogy to the cruder theatrical voice of Hamm (playing the role
of the post-Nietzsche atheist) – 'The bastard! He doesn't exist!'
(*Endgame*, p. 38). What is unique is the supreme fiction that turns
so many disparate ideas, impulses, beliefs and unbeliefs into a new
and personal mythology. This book does not aim to subordinate
the Beckett mythology to any particular environment or system
or ideas, but rather to find the points where the writing and the
ideas connect.

INTRODUCTION

Ireland

The Irish writer in exile can be seen as dwelling in a kind of no-man's-land with persistent echoes of Ireland – in terms of mental and fictional landscape, character and theme and, above all, language and style. Beckett takes after Joyce in this respect, in having preserved the indelible marks of 'the Irish connection', even though he has gone further than Joyce in his separation from his native country: by abandoning Dublin as the specific imaginative setting for his works after his published early collection of stories, *More Pricks than Kicks* (1934), and by deciding to write the trilogy and two of his epoch-making plays in French. Beckett's self-exile thus shows the peculiar intensities of linguistic exile (also seen, in significantly different ways, in the writings of Conrad and Kafka) on top of the culturally 'destabilising' effect of being Irish in the modern world. So when we look at the Irish background, we need to see not only the firm contours of a particular upbringing and landscape, but also the gradual and less distinct transformation of those contours in a long working life spent mostly in Paris.

Like the majority of Anglo-Irish writers (but unlike Joyce) Beckett came from a Protestant and well-to-do middle-class family. He was brought up in a substantial house in leafy Foxrock near Dublin, and received the education of the establishment – at Portora Royal School and Trinity College Dublin – intended by his parents as a preparation for a prosperous career, preferably in the family business. There is no record of a major trauma in his childhood (comparable to the famous conflict between Kafka and his father), though the relationship between a dominating mother and a withdrawn if not already reclusive son is prime material for the biographer. Nor were the child and the young man subjected to the turmoil of war and revolution, though he did watch the fires of the Easter 1916 rebellion from the hills of Dublin, and was moved. The legend, started by Beckett himself, that he was born on Good Friday, 13 April in 1906 cannot be proved; the birth certificate is made out for May that year. But even if he was born on Good Friday, it is the orderliness and the sheltered 'old style' gentility of a pre-First World War childhood, at the relatively quiet edge of the Western world, that strikes one. His early studies were not in any way outstanding – though he did excel at playing cricket. It seems that the scholar and gifted linguist emerged only in his third year at Trinity, and the writer much later. It was his mastery of

French that made his professor recommend him for the much-coveted two-year position as *lecteur* at the Ecole Normale Supérieure in Paris (1928–30), with the expectation that he would grow (or dwindle) into a university professor in romance literature. Beckett started two research projects (including one on Descartes, whose body–mind dualism came to obsess him) and he tried university teaching for a brief spell, only to resign (in 1931), later pleading, with singular integrity: 'how can I teach what I do not understand'. From that date Beckett became just one of the wandering scholars and semi-obscure artistic exiles (settling permanently in Paris in 1937), flanked by a host of dilettanti, with endless experimentation and uncertainty about the ultimate value of anything written.

Can we define what was the most lasting Irish heritage? Added to the habit of travelling with a set of unanswerable questions – theological and metaphysical questions seen existentially – three clusters of deeply ingrained experience stand out: the Dublin theatre, the countryside around Dublin and the language – pure Anglo-Irish, with its lyrical bent and latent instability.

Dublin, a small-scale cultural capital, offered Beckett a substantial introduction to modern drama: the Irish dramatists at the Abbey (including Yeats, Synge and O'Casey), the new European dramatists at the Gate, with melodrama and vaudeville still thriving at lesser theatres (Queen's, Theatre Royal and the Olympia). Beckett thus had the good fortune of being introduced early to three essential elements in his own future drama: Irish (the poetic prose of Synge and the non-realism of Yeats), modern theatricality (including Pirandello) and the popular theatrical tradition. Significantly, Beckett was also fascinated by the cinema: Chaplin, Laurel and Hardy and Harold Lloyd. His mature work includes a filmscript, *Film* (1964), written for Buster Keaton. (For drama generally see 'Contexts for the plays' below.)

The haunting presence of Irish scenery in Beckett's writing – usually described in simple, lyrical language – will be noticed by every reader. But as Beckett does not aim at topographical realism (in any of the works studied here), we may well wonder to what extent that particular 'influence of natural objects' matters in our reading. For example, the island scenery in the final sections of *Malone Dies*, against which are played out the exodus of inmates by boat and the terrible massacre, is unmistakably Irish. It is now possible to be more precise, and track down the course of the boat-trip from Coliemore Harbour to Dalkey Island in the Dublin coastal area: photographs with matching texts from that novel can be gazed at in *The Beckett Country* by Eoin O'Brien.[3] Is this valuable knowledge? Well, the exact particulars of location are clearly quite secondary. But the correspondence of feeling, landscape and language (the associated purity and lyricism) is an essential element in Beckett's writing. So much so that certain novels and plays – including *Molloy*, *Waiting for Godot* and *Krapp's Last Tape* with its 'Vision' on the jetty – transfer fragments of an Irish landscape into the interior landscape of the characters. And to miss that dimension would be to impoverish our reading.

Anglo-Irish as a particular literary language – with its purity of diction mingling with playful rhetoric and wordplay – offers a potential expressiveness beyond the reach of most types of standard twentieth-century (British) English. But it also has a greater potential towards instability, partly through its richness, partly through the insecure 'outsider' self-image of the writers of that language. It is as though the Irish writer were writing a foreign language when writing English – an insight already reached by Stephen Dedalus in Joyce's *A Portrait of the Artist as a Young Man* – or 'a learned language' in Yeats's phrase, or 'struggling with a dead language', like Mrs Rooney in *All that Fall*, Beckett's all-Irish radio play.[4] Then a drive towards hyper-literary expressiveness is accompanied by an acute and often painful consciousness concerning the fragility – or incongruity – of words uttered or written. Even Bernard Shaw's titanic Victorian robustness was not free from a sense of 'absurdity' in his uses of language. Beckett, the most inward and critically language-conscious of all Irish-born writers, moves towards an inner bilingualism even before he came to choose actual bilingualism – that gift which is also a curse, a burden on tongue, pen and consciousness. The mastery of more than one language then reaches a precarious feeling for *all* language as a destructive/creative element to be immersed in. Those who have no direct experience of such a state must imaginatively acquire at least some vicarious language pains. Beckett's inborn language-consciousness was deepened by certain philosophies of language (he is said to have read aloud to Joyce from Mauthner's *Critique of Language*), and by the aesthetic distrust of ordinary language (which Beckett inherited from the French symbolist poets).

The dislocations of language that follow are serious but, given the playfulness of the Anglo-Irish tradition, hardly ever solemn. Humour runs across almost every episode or scene in Beckett's novels and plays. Even when 'it is no laughing matter', a tragicomic language is created that is constantly *at play*, as if acting out the mutilated Nell's response to Nagg's laughter (in one of the ashbin dialogues in *Endgame*, p. 20): 'Nothing is funnier than unhappiness, I grant you that. But – '

Paris

Paris between the two World Wars was still the major centre for innovation in the arts of the West and the cultural melting-pot of all movements as well as of nationals. It was also still a relatively compact and inexpensive place for daily living and writing. Paris in the years after the Second World War experienced the peculiar intensities of a war-tortured survivor – quite distinct from victorious but quiescent London, or from Berlin and Vienna which lay in ruins – spawning popular versions of philosophical existentialism as well as of Marxism, and remaining exceptionally receptive to non-realist writing in fiction as in the theatre. Beckett was fortunate, then, in living through some of the modernist ferments of Paris in the thirties (centred for him in the circle around Joyce and *transition* magazine) and, in the post-war phase, settling down in a 'siege' of seclusion in his old pre-war flat, to write, in French, what can be regarded as the central works of his maturity – the trilogy and the first two plays. It was in many ways a hospitable cultural climate. Although it was still difficult for him to get published or performed in Paris, it would probably have been even more difficult in London (despite the publication of *Murphy* there in 1938), especially as fiction and drama in the Britain of the fifties tended to be dominated by versions of realism (for instance Kingsley Amis, John Osborne).

Intellectual ferment and greater receptivity to his work were, then, the principal windfalls of the Paris milieu. Beckett chose to settle in Paris permanently in 1937, when he was over thirty, after a period of restless *Wanderjahre* spent partly in Germany (drawn by a beautiful cousin and by the culture, not by the rise of Nazism) but mostly in London where he did not thrive. How deliberate was the choice of residence can be seen from his destiny-conscious decision to remain in France when the Second World War broke out. Choosing Paris included a vote against Ireland, at first an escape *from* home, country and religion (the Joycean pattern for exile). But it was also a vote for the provocative conditions just outlined, in a relative writer's haven which could turn into the threat of vanishing 'inside the whale', in Orwell's phrase. What we have to recreate imaginatively here is the fusion, in the Paris of the thirties, of at least three levels of experiment, in living as in writing: the immediate relationship with Joyce, the retrospective critical immersion in Proust, and the ceaseless artistic experimentation, from dada to expressionism and surrealism.

Beckett's relationship with Joyce was more than that of disciple to master, it was in many ways a symbiotic interaction between two very different word-intoxicated artists, between the diffident young apprentice writer and 'the great writer' of the age. They shared a cultural background, an obsessive interest in fictional and verbal patterns pushed to the limits of art, as well as habits of copious drinking and long silences. By the time Beckett met Joyce – during his first stay in Paris, in his years at the Ecole Normale Supérieure (1928–30) – Joyce was working on his ultra-experimental novel *Finnegans Wake* (published in 1939), which aimed at a hybrid super-language made of English words merging with foreign words in a ceaselessly punning dream. Beckett was one of those singled out (with the approval of 'the master') to write a critical defence of Joyce's 'work in progress' in an argument in which the exhaustion or deadness of the (English) language was a cardinal point (see 'Vision and form' below). Beckett's Joycean heritage includes the relentless pursuit of new and extreme positions in writing, sometimes reflected in local experiments such as the unpunctuated final sequence of *The Unnamable* and of the entire text of his last longer fiction, *How It Is* (1961). Nevertheless, Beckett's long-term development can be seen as moving in a counter-Joycean direction – towards greater simplicity, compression and diminishment, as is argued at several points in this study.

Beckett's involvement, as a very subjective critic, with Proust's supreme novel, *Remembrance of Things Past* (*A La Recherche du temps perdu*, 1913–27), is as important in the early Paris years, and in its life-long consequence, as the living relationship with Joyce. For the emphasis that Beckett gave, in the long essay, *Proust* (1931), to Proust's vision and form is emphasis through distortion: intensifying the pessimism in Proust's vision by soaking it in Schopenhauer's 'congenial' philosophy (the inescapable futility of all willing and desiring), and understating Proust's impressionistic delight in the surfaces of a brilliant if flagrantly flawed social world. Implicitly, Beckett has begun to write his own artistic manifesto in the guise of the Proust critic: seeing the novel as 'pure writing' – formal or 'radiographic', the X-ray image replacing the photograph. This prepares the way for Beckett's own aesthetic philosophy and his own experiments, a total fusion of subject matter and expression, vision and form.

Beckett's relationship with revolutionary changes in art – especially with successive movements in the visual arts, expressionism, surrealism, etc. – can be only touched on here. The overall effect was to push the young writer towards non-representational forms of expression, and then towards abstraction. Yet we need to pause and reflect here, for words – unlike colours and shapes, or for that matter sounds – cannot become wholly non-representational or abstract, since they carry the stamp (the referents) of the world's images and concepts into every phrase or sentence. But Beckett was also haunted by certain specific images of avant-garde art, for example, the woman buried in sand in Dali's surrealist film *Le Chien andalou* (1929) may be seen behind the dominant stage image of *Happy Days* (1961).[5]

The Second World War must have deepened Beckett's awareness of suffering and of fearful uncertainty, as well as of the instability of language – to some extent a shared experience among survivors of the war. Beckett was a relatively 'privileged observer' of the war: after joining a Resistance group in Paris and escaping arrest, he lived in hiding in Vichy France, experiencing both danger and long periods of waiting. He must have heard reports of some of the extreme barbarities of the war in occupied France – terror, torture and Nazi deportations – and news of Auschwitz and the other death camps reached France early. One of Beckett's Jewish friends had perished. And while Beckett has never written directly about those extreme experiences (or turned war experience into a moral fable like Golding's *Lord of the Flies*), the imagery of a world that had run its course – a 'corpsed' world – has found its way into *Endgame*. Earlier versions of the text of that play were much nearer to raw experience than the version we know, which has moved towards a universalising myth of negative creation. But we may assume that the play – and much else in Beckett's work – gains some of its power 'to claw' from the dark experiences of the war years.

Thought in post-war France tended to be dominated by Jean-Paul Sartre's existentialism, in its popular and simplified version a 'vision of the world' that sees each self thrown into life without definition, purpose or essence. In its technical version this philosophy explores the total alienation of each person from others (the *other*) and the 'nothingness' of the self as a pure consciousness – separated from the world of things and actions. Such ideas clearly have some relevance to Beckett's vision, and, as already suggested, created a favourable cultural climate for the reception of his post-war work. But, I think, the direct influence of existentialist thought on Beckett has been exaggerated. One might as well argue that Beckett did not 'need' the French versions of existentialism, for he had a version of his own already, made up of a deeply felt sense of loss – in a world where God is absent – and of a medley of philosophical ideas domesticated in his youth. From Descartes came the isolated and solitary self thinking, 'I think therefore I am', starting from a new, anxiously sceptical probing of rationality; from the Irish Bishop Berkeley came the profoundly tragicomic notion that if God does not see me, if nobody sees me, I may not exist; and from Schopenhauer came the vision, akin to Buddhism, that the desiring self does not exist in any 'real' sense, except through suffering the painful consequences of wilful self-assertion. These, and related ideas, filtered through a questioning yet deeply and obsessively feeling temperament, are quite enough 'philosophy' for a writer who is, in any case, not primarily philosophical. Beckett is not presenting ideas but constantly transmuting his own idiosyncratic versions of received ideas into vision – like Dante in *The Divine Comedy*, above all in Purgatory. But, unlike Dante, Beckett has no system of belief; on the contrary, his novels and plays are all written *against* any system.

Beckett's decision to start writing in French and then to become his own translator into English (assisted in the translation of *Molloy*) is probably unique. Conrad could hardly expect to reach a world reading public in his first language, Polish, Koestler in Hungarian, Kafka in Czech; their choice of writing in English or German comprised an element of communicative strategy on top of subtler, private urgencies. But Beckett's choice of French after the war had much more to do with an internal stylistic conflict – the desire to 'write without style', as he once said. That sounds paradoxical for, strictly speaking, writing and style are inseparable Siamese twins. But Beckett admired the relatively neutral 'styleless' writing of the classical period (best seen in the tragedies of Racine) and he wanted to prune away the superabundant expressive potentials of English (Anglo-Irish): the prolific word-stock, wealth of idiom and metaphor, 'the whirling words' of the Hamlet world, with their pressure of incessant private association. French must also have had affinities – in the Parisian cultural environment we have sketched – with Beckett's ever more intense search for experimental and abstract modes of fiction. Not that Beckett's trilogy, for instance, is written in a spare and fully pruned prose style; on the contrary, much of it is dyed in the vigorous, bawdy abundance of a Rabelais as well as in the parodic playfulness of a Sterne. But, starting with *The Unnamable*, French may well be the language most appropriate to Beckett's increasingly abstract fiction (even though Beckett's translations create idioms and rhythms that have the force of 'original' English), while the dialogue of the plays is, arguably, at its most expressive in English. At all events, after *Endgame* the majority of play-texts were written in English. For proper study at least one text should be read bilingually and comparatively so as to trace, with some precise examples in mind, the tensions and challenges of self-translation (for example, *'Happy Days' and 'Oh Les Beaux Jours'* – *A Bilingual Edition*, edited by James Knowlson, London, 1978).

Vision and form: the tightening knot

From the start, Beckett inwardly appropriated the most vital creative principles of the modernist writer: the need for innovation, and with it the need for constantly re-creating form and language within and for each new work. In the criticism of his youth – the self-defining essays on Joyce and Proust – Beckett took up key positions on verbal art, which illuminate not only the genesis but also the future growth of his ideas *on* writing. Those ideas were put into creative practice, gradually but radically, in the continuously changing fictional and dramatic work, following a curve of ever more intense compression or 'lessness' – a principle of 'less is more'.

In a learned yet lively defence of Joyce's experimental and punning language in *Finnegans Wake* (then incomplete and still known as 'Work in Progress'), Beckett defended the need to renew or reinvigorate the language. The immediacy of words – their sounds and their hieroglyph-like picture language – was to be released in and through new writing. For the English language had become 'abstracted to death' – something like a dead language (like medieval Latin). By contrast, in Joyce's language-in-the-making 'the language is drunk. The very words are tilted and effervescent.' Beckett was carried into a resonant manifesto in defence of this kind of verbal expressiveness:

Here form *is* content, content *is* form. You complain that this stuff is not written in English. It is not written at all. It is not to be read – or rather

11

it is not only to be read. It is to be looked at and listened to. His writing
is not *about* something; *it is that something itself.* ('Dante . . . Bruno.
Vico . . . Joyce' in *Our Exagmination Round His Factification for Incamination
of Work in Progress* (1929), London, 1972, p. 14)

This sounds like an indirect manifesto of his own aims as a
writer. Certainly writing for Beckett always 'is itself' and not
'about something' in the sense of a subject that can be separated
out – as an independent statement, action or narrative – from
the way it is expressed in words within a re-created form or genre.
On this point Beckett was in tune not only with Joyce, but with
the various symbolist theories of poetic language, notably
Mallarmé's 'Crise de vers' (1886–95). Such a post-symbolist idea
of language is opposed not only to the vulgarly materialistic
language of commerce, journalism and ape-like chattering, but
ultimately to representational language – versions of the view
that language mirrors the world (mimesis). The contrary concept
holds that in poetic or fictional writing (both words used, across
the various genres, to signify imaginative writing), language functions in a self-mirroring and self-authenticating way. The act of
writing is then primarily a re-working, a re-creation, of words for
images and sounds, as the painter works with shapes and colours
and the composer with sounds. (It is again possible to object that
language is different: resisting full abstraction and not to be
severed from the human, personal and social world, the outward-
pointing connotations that our words, phrases, and even our syntax and punctuation carry.)

Beckett's intense wrestling with words – with questions of expression, form, 'style', with *how* to write – should not be mistaken for
a cool, rational, 'formalist' idea of verbal art. On the contrary,
from the start Beckett's search for words is inseparable from a
search for the traces of meaning within our experiences of
diminished meaning. So far from being a latter-day aestheticist –
a practitioner of 'art for art's sake – a tremendous concern for
modes of being and suffering is the force that drives his experiments in writing. In the long essay *Proust* (1931) – which
argues as strongly against realist or photographic literature as the
essay on Joyce – Beckett writes, as if balancing a tension of
opposites:

For Proust, as for the painter, style is more a question of vision than of
technique. [. . .]

For Proust the quality of language is more important than any system of
ethics or aesthetics. Indeed he makes no attempt to dissociate form from
content. The one is a concretion of the other, the revelation of a world.

(Proust (1931), London, 1965, p. 88)

'The equation is never simple', in the words that open *Proust,* but
these quotations point to something like a complex modern version
of the cryptic equation of 'truth' and 'beauty' in the concluding lines
of Keats's 'Ode on a Grecian Urn'. The language *is* more important
than any *system* of ethics or aesthetics in Beckett's work (more so
than in Proust, it may be affirmed). Yet 'the question of vision' –
and 'the revelation of a world' – is present in every work. It is present in the compassionate ending of his early near-realist story
'Dante and the Lobster' (written as early as 1932):

Well, thought Belacqua, it's a quick death [for the lobster being boiled
alive], God help us all.

It is not.   *(More Pricks than Kicks,* London, 1970, p. 21)

It is still present in the play written some fifty years later, in the
compressed soliloquy of a dying woman in *Rockaby* (1981), where
the life-long isolation and the final solitude of the woman is
expressed in a simple, mostly monosyllabic, rhythmic 'cradling
dirge':

> so in the end
> close of a long day
> went down
> let down the blind and down
> right down
> into the old rocker
> and rocked
> rocked
> saying to herself
> no
> done with that
> *(Collected Shorter Plays,* London, 1984, pp. 281–2)

Typically guarding against pathos or sentimentality, the voice
then goes on to curse – 'fuck life' – before the elegiac rocking
movement closes.

The vision is centrally present in the – presumably autobiographical – tape-recording to young Krapp, re-played and impatiently interrupted by old Krapp in his isolated den:

clear to me at last that the dark I have always struggled to keep under is
in reality my most –   *(Krapp's Last Tape,* London, 1958, p. 15)

'My most' . . . What? Creative source, or something like that: the recognition that the dark (which includes despair and recurrent nihilism) yields a kind of light, the acute sense of impotence releases a kind of strength. Along with this vision – corresponding to an actual experience of Beckett – goes the determination to work through that terrible failure of words, which is one of the obsessional threads in *The Unnamable* – an unstable self trapped among ceaselessly sounded but un-definable and inexpressible names.

That aspect of the dark, the total loss of certainty concerning both the self and its language(s), becomes a powerful negative/ creative force that drives Beckett's work towards the limits of art. An extreme 'aesthetics of failure' is the conceptual counterpart of that vision, formulated in a series of paradoxes on art in Beckett's Dialogues with Duthuit (the post-war editor of *transition*, the once-famous avant-garde journal published in Paris). These challenging paradoxes must be included here, for they represent a radical shift in Beckett's post-war concept of art. Most of his early statements on literature are, like the ones already quoted, concerned with the fairly typical modernist (but also romantic) question of how to make writing fully alive when the language (or the dominant culture) is dying. Thus when Beckett wants words to be more alive, to present pictures like hieroglyphs, he is after something comparable to what Ezra Pound wanted in his imagist phase, extolling the Chinese ideogram. Again 'the *radiographical* quality' (my emphasis) of observations (*Proust*, p. 83) is something Virginia Woolf would have approved of, with her search for a luminous, non-descriptive prose in her essay *Modern Fiction* (1925). But in the post-war years Beckett moved towards a far more radical position – gradually transferring to the art of writing certain creed-like statements on the very different art of non-figurative painting, a propos of the work of his painter friends Tal Coat, Masson and Bram van Velde:

B: I speak of an art turning from it in disgust, weary of puny exploits, weary of pretending to be able, of being able, of doing a little better the same old thing . . .
D: And preferring what?
B: The expression that there is nothing to express, nothing with which to express, nothing from which to express, no power to express, no desire to express, together with the obligation to express.
     (*Three Dialogues*, in *transition* 1949, no. 5; quoted from *Proust*, p. 103)

Beckett is here moving into total scepticism about the value, and even the possibility, of artistic expression. It amounts to a creative paradox, a double paradox. The attraction of the inexpressible – saying the unsayable, against a felt reality of nothing to be said – is matched by the irrepressible 'obligation to express', rather than choosing the total silence of blank pages. The second paradox may well spring from an urgent, primary experience, comparable to what a certain poetic tradition invoked in such words as listening to an inner voice, the daimon, the Muse, 'dictations from the Almighty' (Blake).

Listening to irrepressible voices – Beckett's mature and late work has been a response to such listening. At the same time the intense sense of failure – of art and of language – *has* come to function like a creative principle: the writer's impotence is transformed by and within a ceaseless work-in-progress. The vision of a cosmic and human run-down (a de-creation) and the *lessening* resources of writing converge in specific and unique created works. The paradoxical dark light, the dynamic immobility and the rich poverty of the texts spring from that unifying creativity.

I

THE PLAYS

1

Contexts for the plays

Beckett's plays, once regarded as 'anti-plays' (in a superficial yet telling cliché), can now be seen as inherently dramatic. More than that, the often hyper-literary fiction was followed and cut across by fundamentally theatrical, stage-oriented plays – constantly using yet transforming popular as well as literary dramatic conventions. Vividly concrete theatre images and figures dominate the plays: from the entrance of the whip-cracking Pozzo leading Lucky in harness, to the extra-terrestrial voices chanting from urns in *Play*. Starting with *Waiting for Godot*, Beckett's plays have, aided by performance, become his most accessible works (which is one reason for starting this study with the plays, even though chronologically they are preceded by the early and mature fiction). In a relatively short period of creativity – *Godot* was written, in French, in 1948, but brought to fame only by the New York and London productions of 1954 and 1955, while *Happy Days*, the last of the full-length plays, was first performed as long ago as 1961 – Beckett created a radically new kind of theatre. That innovative art embraces all the elements of theatre – new types of play, stage metaphor, character, dialogue, visual and sound effects. Even the potentially disembodied 'I'-voices of isolated soliloquisers appear embodied in the time present and the dynamics of the stage. The dramatised voices of Krapp or Winnie or the three voices of *Play* mark a fundamental generic difference from any solo narrator in the trilogy. Other writers who had come from fiction to drama – like Chekhov and Pirandello – started from the realistic short story, which was nearer to the traditional idea of the 'dramatic'.

Beckett's drama has changed our very idea of the dramatic, of what is possible within the limits of a dramatic performance. Apart from the constant paring away of the spatial dimensions of drama, a 'timeless' or circular structure of action has entered the spectrum of dramatic forms, against the long dominance of the logic of time in various plot-centred versions. Within a non-sequential play structure, an inward-moving dialogue has made us attentive to the moment-by-moment ripple effect of words (and silences) in the theatre. In sum, a new type of poetic drama in

19

prose has been brought into being, an achievement that surpasses, in several respects, the dramatic work of major modern poets – including Yeats and Eliot – and most of the symbolist and expressionist plays of the first half of this century.

The radical innovations in dramatic form did not come 'out of the blue' either in Beckett's inner development as a writer or in the movements of modern European drama. Two unpublished apprentice works (surviving only as manuscripts) show a search for creative opportunities through play-writing, and a commitment exceeding the lighter interest suggested by Beckett himself (who claimed that the Godot play was written as 'a kind of game', a relaxation from the terrible labour of writing the trilogy). *Human Wishes* (1937) is a play fragment on the ageing Dr Johnson, of all people (less surprising if we remember Johnson's melancholy, his fear of death): a potentially realistic play, based on copious historical documentation, but one that already shows a high frequency of *silences* in the stage directions, together with the counterpointing of word and gesture – two unmistakable features of the mature Beckett plays. *Eleuthéria* (1947) – the Greek title means freedom – still has 'the basic structure of the well-made play, but irrelevant characters derive from vaudeville'.[1] It is surprising to find such a relatively conventional and diffuse play written only two years before *Godot* (though it is said that the producer, Roger Blin, was prepared to stage the earlier play but chose *Godot* instead, because it required only five actors). Since Beckett has consistently withheld these play-texts from publication or performance, we need be aware of them only as trial runs before the leap into radically new visions and forms.

Similarly, we may point to affinities between Beckettian and earlier types of modern drama without arguing that Beckett's drama derives in a straight line from any particular dramatist. (The influence-hunting criticism has been overdone for, beyond a certain point, it does not illuminate the genesis, still less the 'originality', of any one play.) As stated in two earlier contexts, 'Ireland' and 'Paris', Beckett had the good fortune of seeing a wide variety of play-types: he had seen some of the key plays of the Irish dramatic movement (alongside music hall, melodrama and the silent cinema) as well as of the continental innovators, including Maeterlinck (widely admired at the turn of the century, in part for his experiments with silence and unspoken dialogue in plays such as *The Intruder* (*L'Intruse* (1890)), Strindberg and

Pirandello. In the formative years, when art was experienced upon the pulses, Beckett caught the fever of innovation from various avant-garde movements of the interwar period – the expressionists, surrealists and dadaists – without becoming a devotee of any one 'ism'. What mattered was the general thrust towards artistic experimentation which, however varied and multi-directional, went against the grain, and beyond the forms and languages, of naturalism and realism – in short, away from the photographic and towards the radiographic.[2]

The new Irish drama of Synge and Yeats offered significant images and obsessions – as well as verbal experiments – which are echoed in Beckett's drama. Synge's *The Well of the Saints* (1905) presents a mutually dependent blind couple awaiting a cure that is to lead to disappointment, to seeing an ugly world (a situational affinity with *Godot*). Moreover, Synge tried to forge a poetic Anglo-Irish prose dialogue (against the 'pallid' language of Ibsen) – an aim inherited by Beckett, though he avoids Synge's sometimes ostentatiously local Irish English. Yeats's lyric mode is present in Beckett's theatre, partly through quotation (for instance, Winnie quoting in *Happy Days*, 'I call to the eye of the mind' . . . from Yeats's play *At the Hawk's Well*), or through the formal and spiritual traces of the Japanese Noh play mediated by Yeats.[3] (Beckett may have been haunted by the spirit but not by the spiritualism of Yeats, though the voices crying from limbo in *Play* sound ghostly.)

However, all these elements (a legacy of themes and words tending to lyricism) gain much of their vitality from a conscious return to the theatre *as* theatre: using the bare boards, the empty space. Then every gesture and word counts, often pointing to both stage and audience and the internal elements of a play, as in Hamm's 'warming up for my final soliloquy' and the amusing interruption of the otherwise inescapable course of suffering by a reference to the 'dialogue' that alone keeps the characters on stage (see chapter 3, pp. 61–6). Little attempt is made – that is less and less attempt as Beckett's drama evolves – to 'create an illusion of reality'; the play as play is an axiomatic starting point and a self-mirroring world. However, Beckett's play-world is not as systematically theatrical as that of Pirandello in the celebrated *Six Characters in Search of an Author* (1921), for Beckett has no use for the play-within-the-play as an elaborate framework or for any explicit rhetoric of role-playing, making a character explain rationally the nature of his irrationality. Beckett's theatricality is more limited yet also more radically anti-rational: moving away from any public explanation or telling of a character's 'personal experience', towards the raw exposure of pseudo-couples (in the first two plays) and the inner drama in isolated minds.

It is remarkable to what extent the inwardness of such a drama is theatricalised. One source of Beckett's gifts for theatricality is, undoubtedly, the popular theatre: the English music hall, especially the cross-talk and serious clowning of paired male comedians, and later that of the solo performer. From the hat-tricks of Gogo and Didi to the clown-face of Krapp and the semi-farcical moaning of adulterers from somewhere beyond the grave in *Play*, the popular dramatic element is subordinated to an overall tragicomic vision. An all-pervasive gallows humour safeguards the plays from any portentousness that might otherwise burden a dramatic metaphor – the apocalyse of Hamm's corpsed kingdom is threatened by a flea that might still procreate and thus spoil the purity of an extinct world. The drive towards compression and formal coherence also helps to make the plays seem paradoxically light and exhilarating. (A certain looseness of structure has often been the hall-mark of symbolist plays: even Strindberg, a master of construction in his realistic plays, tended to let in the chaos of the world in the structure of a play like *A Dream Play* (1902) and *The Ghost Sonata* (1907), a play that Beckett had seen in Paris, though he has denied its influence.) Any 'imitation' of the world's chaos by the structure of the work gives way in Beckett's plays to an economy of form that corresponds to an urgency of vision – the chaos of the world mediated by clarity.

This study focuses repeatedly on such correspondences, in particular plays. The cyclic or circular pattern that takes the place of the 'lines' and 'curves' of nearly all Western drama is a significant example. A run-down cycle 'imitates' a diminishing human condition – no more carrots . . . no more bicycles . . . no more Nature. It also suspends our 'normal' expectations within time: of a line of development (historical, biographical, etc.) with inevitable climaxes. Further, when the structure of action is nearer to a spiral moving inward than to an arrow moving onward, then the present moment – the here and now of action, the acting on the stage – becomes all-important. By contrast, any recall of past action (which looms as large in Greek tragedy as in Ibsen-type realism) becomes shadowy or is barely alluded to. (In *Play* alone do the three figures speaking from the urns endlessly rehearse versions of a story from their past.) Moreover, characters caught in a run-down cycle do not aspire to a future – they know that they do not have a future. Yet the recurrent allusions to some pending event (the coming of Godot, the ending of the endgame, etc.) create a tension in terms of stage time – we might call it suspense, though not in its thriller sense. 'Something is taking its course', and is moving relentlessly towards some continuously receding end. It has been likened to the curve mathematicians call asymptotic: all the time approximating but never reaching the graph's bottom line.

The uncertainties, the non-resolutions, the gaps and impasses within the pattern of action in a Beckett play all work dramatically – and so do the moments of philosophical reflection and the lyrical still points. And, paradoxically, the later plays tend to become more theatrical, though less substantially 'flesh and blood'. The plays get nearer to pure theatre, in the sense that they could not function in any other genre or medium; witness the central image of Winnie buried up to the waist/the neck at the centre of her dialogue-imitating rhapsodic monologue in *Happy Days*. Correspondingly, we have a new type of play-text here in which extensive, significant and fully theatrical stage directions (that is, directions that refer to gesture, movement, visual and auditive effects, and not to psychological or social circumstances as, for example, in the copiously discursive stage directions of a Shaw play) are woven into the dialogue. *Happy Days* is a play that foreshadows the miniature plays Beckett started writing in the seventies (see chapter 5, pp. 160–3, and Concluding reflections), with their ultimate compression of soliloquising voices within a nevertheless living theatre, where 'the words that remain' call out for performance as much as a musical score. It is impossible to foresee what posterity will make of this inexorable inner development of Beckett's drama, but for our time it is unique and unlikely to be emulated in the same forms.

2

Waiting for Godot

It is not surprising that fourteen hundred convicts of San Quentin penitentiary responded enthusiastically to a performance of Beckett's play (in 1957) – completely strange yet meaningful to them. They could draw on their own experience of waiting, the empty kind of waiting where 'nothing to think about' is a permanent threat, and every happening offers both a promise and a disillusioning repetition of the daily round. They also had fewer preconceptions about what constitutes a well-plotted play than did the literary and theatre-going public of the time.

We are not in the situation of the prisoners of San Quentin; and the risk, in our time and especially for the new reader, is a second-hand or learned response to a 'great modern classic' (an examination set book), over-burdened with often far-fetched commentary. The best starting point for critical discussion is still the immediate experience of the play, guided by searching questions concerning both the text and its context. The stage is almost empty, stripped, as hardly ever since Shakespeare, to present only the bare boards and one tree, which can suggest almost anything from the tree of life to all that is left of 'Nature' in a deserted and desolate landscape. The stage is the stage, it is also a road. (It could be a round stage suggesting the circus, but the stage directions do not ask for that.) The opening sequence defines the situation of Vladimir and Estragon clearly enough for a play that is to use 'uncertainty' as an element of composition. Both characters are ageing and weary; they appear to be inseparably linked as a pair, in the symbiotic love–hate relationship of a couple; they are usually dressed as bowler-hatted literary tramps, though the stage directions do not state this; they are also like performing comedians, the straight man and his stooge in cross-talk. Their strong physical presence is underlined by talk of physical discomfort and pain – Estragon's boot problem, Vladimir's urination problem. Metaphysical uncertainty is suggested by their speculative talk about time, place and the purpose of their waiting, about what *is* happening, what might have happened (should they have jumped from the top of the Eiffel Tower some fifty years ago?) and what might happen.

24

Their speech is a mixture of the formal ('Nothing to be done') and the colloquial; the minimally simple and the rhetorical, with a sprinkling of Irishisms ('Get up till I embrace you') and literary or biblical allusion ('Hope deferred maketh the something sick, who said that?'). The collision of levels and styles is controlled, good-humoured and darkly humorous (tragicomic) from the opening scene on.

Action in non-action

The act of waiting makes us aware of an indirect and ambivalent kind of action that promises an end in the sense of purpose as well as conclusion. Waiting, both in life and in drama, can involve a whole range of experience, from a sense of paralysis to fruitful silence, the empty or the anxious mind trying to cope by inventing distractions. The suspense of melodrama and farce, the long postponements of comedy and the prolonged quest of tragedy (the procrastinations of Hamlet for example) all constitute patterns of waiting.

In Beckett's play, the pattern of waiting is an ingenious combination of expectations and let-downs, of uncertainty and of gradual run-down without end. The expectations of Estragon and Vladimir seem to be both limitless and irrational; and the various climaxes and pseudo-climaxes, or non-arrivals, do not change their condition. But the protagonists, and the audience, are being 'kept going' by playful variations in the pattern of waiting, with uncertainties of meaning and destination. For example, early on we hear Vladimir's speculations on the traditional hope of being saved:

VLADIMIR: It'll pass the time. (*Pause.*) It was two thieves crucified at
   the same time as our Saviour. One –
ESTRAGON: Our what?
VLADIMIR: Our Saviour. Two thieves. One is supposed to have been
   saved and the other . . . (*he searches for the contrary of being saved*)
   . . . damned.
ESTRAGON: Saved from what?
VLADIMIR: Hell.
                   (p. 12)

['Hell' is later vehemently exchanged for 'death' by Vladimir.]

The whole sequence sounds tentative and open-ended, both in performance and when examined critically. Only one out of three evangelists tells of one thief being saved, and if the silence of the others is a kind of truth, then both thieves may have been damned. The reader/spectator feels that the uncertainty concerning one of the thieves is transferred to the speakers, but without the firm equation we find in *The Pilgrim's Progress* type allegory. It is a haunting and universal image, like a medieval triptych of the Crucifixion with the central panel, the Christ picture, missing. But a direct Christian symbolic interpretation would not be warranted. The allusion to some remote possibility of 'being saved' is not excluded by the text; it reverberates as a concern, an anxious questioning – without nihilistic parody.

The presence of the tree offers no consolation; assumed to be a dead willow by Vladimir, it cannot, at this point, serve even as a landmark. On the contrary, it prompts the first symptoms of fear: being at the wrong place at the wrong time, waiting in vain (pp. 14–15). The black humour of trying to identify a meeting-place where landmarks get blurred, or trying to distinguish between today and yesterday when all the days of the week merge in 'sameness', defines the first movement of the play. Estragon's *if*'s ('And if he doesn't come?', 'If he came yesterday and we weren't here you may be sure he won't come again today') and his *until* ('until he comes') present the anxieties within this act of waiting at an early stage. The risk of waiting in vain is also emphasised early in the play by the failure of an attempt to clarify the inexorable conditions supposedly set by the supposed Mr. Godot. In the course of a long dialogue 'canter' concerning Godot (pp. 18–19), Vladimir is forced to admit, with scathing irony, that they no longer have any 'rights' – 'We got rid of them' ('waived them' in the first edition, French *bazardés*). Meanwhile, every noise brings fear: the wind in the reeds or a shout may usher in the coming of Godot.

So the terrible cry that precedes the arrival of Pozzo and Lucky creates the illusion of Godot's arrival, not just for the protagonists, but for a first audience as well. It turns out to be a supreme diversion, in the double scene of amusing distraction and enforced detour. Throughout this long and centrally placed play-within-the-play the direct act of waiting is suspended: attention shifts to the doings of Pozzo and Lucky, the lord of the waste, and his shrivelled carrier, dancer, thinker, speaker. The abandoned road suddenly takes on the appearance of the old highway of picaresque fiction (as in *Tom Jones*, say): *anything* might happen here, monster-like creatures can traverse this road and enact a cruel spectator sport, watched by Estragon and Vladimir. The compulsions of the long process of waiting are almost forgotten despite Pozzo's occasional speculations about the identity and demands of this personage: 'Godet . . . Godot . . . Godin' (pp. 29, 36). The name of Godot is hushed up with ironic apologies for having taken Pozzo for 'him': ('Personally, I wouldn't even know him if I saw him.' / 'That's to say . . . you understand . . . the dusk . . . the strain . . . waiting . . . I confess . . . I imagined . . . for a second . . .'). At this stage the deepening uncertainty about Godot's appearance and whereabouts tells the audience, significantly, that anyone who comes might be taken for the one who is expected. Thus the act of waiting, which keeps suggesting a quest, has been undertaken on the flimsiest supposition, a casual invitation from an absent host.

The terrible interlude of Pozzo and Lucky 'passes the time' but changes nothing. Soon, the first appearance of the Boy (before the end of Act I) re-enacts and sums up the uncertainties of waiting. In a quiet ritual the Boy appears, like a Messenger in Greek drama, but without any message. For a tense moment, it sounds as if some oracle might be disclosed: 'You have a message from Mr. Godot?' / 'Yes, sir.' But the little scene that begins by miming the gesture of a revelation, shifts into an inconclusive cross-examination:

Silence.

VLADIMIR: You work for Mr. Godot?
BOY: Yes, sir.
VLADIMIR: What do you do?
BOY: I mind the goats, sir.
VLADIMIR: Is he good to you?
BOY: Yes, sir.
VLADIMIR: He doesn't beat you?
BOY: No, sir, not me.
VLADIMIR: Whom does he beat?
BOY: He beats my brother, sir.
VLADIMIR: Ah, you have a brother?
BOY: Yes, sir.
VLADIMIR: What does he do?
BOY: He minds the sheep, sir.
VLADIMIR: And why doesn't he beat you?
BOY: I don't know, sir.
VLADIMIR: He must be fond of you.
BOY: I don't know, sir.

Silence.

(p. 51)

The light fusion of myth and realism (trying to track down an elusive person or possibility) sounds 'possible', soothing, almost affirmative. Since no message *has* come down to them, Vladimir will send a message to Mr. Godot: 'Tell him . . . tell him you saw us. (*Pause.*) You did see us, didn't you?' For the moment, the inconclusive ritual has at least confirmed the existence of Estragon and Vladimir. In that sense the waiting has not been in vain, so far. In the controlled uncertainty of the concluding dialogue of the first act, the Christ image returns ('ESTRAGON: All my life I have compared myself to him'), along with Estragon's naming of the suicide rope, and vague memories of an earlier existence, some time (fifty years ago perhaps), some place (by the Rhône?). Estragon's serio-comic longing for separation ('We weren't made for the same road') gives way to the curtain image (*They do not move*): separation is both wanted and feared; movement is desired but paralysed; the end is far from ending.

The second act, with its cycle of repetitions and variations, dramatises the ultimate problem of waiting: 'passing the time' without total lethargy. Recharging the batteries of patience is as hard for Estragon and Vladimir as keeping non-action 'going' is for the dramatist.

First, the sense of an 'eternal return' is dramatised by Vladimir's opening round-song ('And dug the dog a tomb') which might as well go on for ever. Then the recognition of Estragon by Vladimir, repeating variants of some phrases from the opening of Act I ('Come here till I embrace you'), also suggests a ritual without end. By contrast, the sudden flowering of the tree, and later Pozzo's blindness and Lucky's dumbness, are *new* events which underline the relentless onward march of time. Yet the movement of time is stilled, or slowed down to the point of stasis, by the sense of a perpetual present, by the circularity of the action (see pp. 42–6 below), and by the self-conscious efforts of the protagonists to bury time. We watch Estragon and Vladimir jointly trying to tinker with the wheels of time, so to speak. But their perceptions of time are comically opposed (pp. 59–62). For Vladimir, today is firmly 'today', a new day, after the passage of a night spent in solitude but with a degree of happiness. (Perhaps 'happiness' is inseparable from greeting the day as new and distinct, as Winnie is to do in *Happy Days*.) By contrast, Estragon denies the separateness of today and yesterday, and claims a kind of total amnesia; the supposed passage of one night has wiped out his memory of the tree, the attempted suicide, and the arrival of Pozzo and Lucky. All that remains is a blur and a pain. The place itself is not recognised by Estragon; when challenged, he furiously rejects the 'scenery' as a 'muckheap'. The depressed sense of sameness – loss of feeling *for* time and place – has turned the Macon country into the Cackon country, a place of dirt, panic, or general sickness.

The act of waiting makes urgent demands even when those who wait are beginning to lose their feeling of urgency. Their situation may not be hopeless, may even be euphoric – for a moment. Early in the second act, Vladimir invites Estragon (still smarting from being beaten at night, and other grievances) to a little ceremony affirming mutual happiness:

VLADIMIR: Say, I am happy.
ESTRAGON: I am happy.
VLADIMIR: So am I.
ESTRAGON: So am I.
VLADIMIR: We are happy.
ESTRAGON: We are happy. (*Silence.*) What do we do now, now that we are happy?
VLADIMIR: Wait for Godot. (*Estragon groans. Silence.*) Things have changed since yesterday.
ESTRAGON: And if he doesn't come?
VLADIMIR: (*After a moment of bewilderment.*) We'll see when the time comes. (*Pause.*) (p. 60)

Being 'happy', this ironic ritual shows, is not a compulsive need like 'waiting', which has some of the qualities of a total commitment. The prospect of being disappointed time after time – after some fifty years – is shrugged off with that cliché of the optimistic clown: 'We'll see when the time comes.'

The act of waiting becomes both more playful and more desperate in Act II. Self-congratulations for 'success' alternate with cries of anguished lamentation. In a fine succession of verbal games (pp. 62–77) Estragon and Vladimir try out improvised poetry (the line-by-line lyrical repartee on 'the dead voices' / 'like leaves' / 'like sands'); they try contradicting each other, asking further questions, recapitulating the already fading lore of 'yesterday', testing memory, testing the sun and the moon, the cosmos, and, nearer home, the continuity of experience: Estragon's leg-wound and the reality of his boots (the black pair has been replaced by a brown one, as if a practical joker had come in the night). Further games of self-distraction follow: eating a radish (there are no more carrots), trying on the boots, trying to sleep, the hat-game with Lucky's 'thinking' hat, and finally improvising their own acts ('I'll do Lucky, you do Pozzo'), a cursing match, a ritual of reconciliation, and exercises ('doing the tree'). It is this kind of inventiveness that earns Estragon's self-approval:

> We don't manage too badly, eh Didi, between the two of us? [. . .] We always find something, eh Didi, to give us the impression we exist?(p. 69)

The 'merry' games of self-distraction are cut across by an intermittent cry. At its simplest, we hear Estragon's repeated 'Ah' as an increasingly desperate response to the 'we are waiting for Godot' refrain. While Estragon is troubled by his nightmare, Vladimir begins to find the long silences unendurable ('This is awful!') and in a fit of despair he has a vision of corpses in a charnel-house world (pp. 63–4). At nightfall he is restless and in pain; and Estragon is filled with the ultimate dread of not knowing what to do ('What'll we do, what'll we do!', p. 71). Vladimir's hallucinations ('It's Godot! At last!') are getting wilder, while Estragon feels trapped in hell, with no exit. Again, the comedy – the games and inprovisations – is counterpointed by the terror of nothing to do and nothing to think about. In this predicament, Estragon calls out to his companion: 'Do you think God sees me?'; staggering and brandishing his fists, he shouts words resembling the mass: 'God have pity on me!' The cycle of hope and despair – and the evening of waiting in the theatre – is about to run down when the second 'diversion' of Pozzo and Lucky brings ironic 'reinforcements', a fit occasion for Vladimir's pastiche ceremonial speech:

> We are no longer alone, waiting for the night, waiting for Godot, waiting for . . . waiting.   (p. 77)

The celebration is mocked by the impact of the second Pozzo and Lucky action, which turns Estragon and Vladimir once more into stage spectators (and vaudeville actors) endlessly playing off, and playing against, Pozzo's cries of help.

Their offers to help peter out in chattering and clowning and in Vladimir's rhetoric ('Let us do something while we have the chance!'). In the midst of this farcical episode, Pozzo's revelation that he is blind and that Lucky is dumb, and his speech on time and the simultaneity of birth and death ('They give birth astride of the grave', p. 89) echo the tones of traditional tragedy. Vladimir in his 'waking sleep' speech seems to remember the 'astride of a grave' image as he speculates on a possibly infinite series of observers watching each other ('At me too someone is looking'). Both the Pozzo and the Vladimir speeches transform the action into a dream-like state and contribute to the experience of a 'timeless time' which is prevalent in the whole play.

The final movement turns on the second coming of the Boy as messenger. The repetition, with variations of the end of Act I, exploits the deeply rooted human interest in patterns of anticipation, return and disappointment. Once again there is a cumulative sense of anti-climax ('No, Sir' / 'Yes, Sir' / Mr. Godot 'does nothing, Sir'; he has a white beard). Yet the slow cross-examination with its long silences creates a new encounter, and the news of *nothing* still sounds as if it were about *something* important. The suicide attempt is repeated too, with Estragon forgetting that he has pulled his trousers down – a broad vaudeville act placed riskily near the end. The ending parallels Act I, counterpointing 'Yes, let's go' (this time spoken by Estragon) with *they do not move*, and suggesting that repetition could be endless – an infinite series of action/non-action sequences.

The account just given of endless 'waiting' as a type of action (so hard for the Western mind to conceptualise even when it has been experienced) should serve as a basis for interpreting the play. Thus we should avoid those eager leaps of ideological interpretation that reduce the play at a premature stage of reception: Existentialist (Godot shows man lost in a world after the death of God); Marxist (only the alienation of a late capitalist society, coupled with the hysteria of the cold war, can have produced such a work, where man ceases to be a political animal); Freudian (Gogo represents the *id*, Didi the *ego*); Christian (the play is a parable on man's need for salvation).

When such an overall view is imposed on the play before the complexities and ambiguities of the text have been explored, understanding is diminished. At a later stage the reductive views may at least serve as 'debating points', remembering that they reflect, beyond aspects of the play, the divided state of our culture. That can be seen in these pairs of opposites (all taken from the first fifteen years of the play's reception):

'the artistic portrayal of man's absurd existence as it appears to Beckett' (Rechstein, 1969)
'an existentialist play [arguing] against the assumption of an image that drains off the energy of stark human responsibility (Hoffman, 1962)

'a profoundly anti-Christian play' (C. Chadwick)
'a Christian play' (Ronald Gray, 1957, among others)

'an atheist existentialist play' (*Times Literary Supplement*, 13 April 1956)

'a modern morality play on permanent Christian themes' (G. S. Fraser, *Times Literary Supplement*, 10 February 1956)

'a picture of unrelieved blackness' (G. E. Wellwarth, 1961)

'a modern classic affirming man's dignity and ultimate salvation' (L. J. Marinello, 1963)[1]

Such views, with their ping-pong ball way of coming down as plus and minus signs, are best approached through fundamental questions: Is the act of waiting purposeful, can it be seen as humanly rewarding? Is there a centre within the stream of uncertainty in the play? (These questions will be discussed later from the point of view of character and vision.)

Beckett himself shares the distaste of all modernist writers for attempts at 'expounding' a literary work explicitly, regarding 'content' and 'form', meaning and the language of the work, as inseparable. *Waiting for Godot* was once said by Beckett to be 'a play that is striving to avoid definition'. The impulse to explain what the dramatist 'means', to clarify uncertainties, to impose the author's view upon the work (so strongly present in the plays of Shaw, who then provided long prefaces expounding his 'meaning') is abhorrent to Beckett. On the contrary, this play is written in such a way that it cannot be pinned down, can only be opened up with further questions. Some kind of 'principle of uncertainty' is built into the fabric of the play at every level; all is implicit.

We have seen that the act of waiting as dramatised in this play is not the kind that would 'normally' pass for goal-directed activity in a Western culture imbued with classical, humanist, socialist and, increasingly, technological goals. A certain type of reader will react to the play with a wish to reject it, on first exposure. Apart from seeing the play's patterns of waiting as pointless, the impatient Western activist will object that the playful improvisations and digressions, which constitute entire scenes in the play, have no centre. Further, as the name Godot is in the title and is constantly being dangled before us in the famous refrain 'We are waiting for Godot', and as the name happens to suggest the name of God (though only in English, the evocative pun cannot work in the French text, or in any translation) much time can be spent speculating on the identity and whereabouts of this Mr. X. Attempts at defining Godot perpetually defeat Estragon and Vladimir; yet all those attempts cumulatively give a centre to the process of waiting. In other words, the endless repetitive tricks for passing the time are highly structured around one object. It is possible to stress the *for* in the waiting for . . .: to see the purpose of action in two men with a mission, not to be deflected from their compulsive task. In that light the tramps acquire some of the characteristics of the quest hero, parodied yet still striving after 'something' infinite. They may be deluded, but they connect with certain literary figures (Don Quixote?) and general human experience.

If the status of Godot remains uncertain from beginning to end, as the *object* of waiting Mr. X acquires values and becomes more and more recognisable. The uncertain figure is gradually endowed with strange/familiar features, personal (cruel or patient) and impersonal (beyond the human world, doing 'nothing'). Through being constantly talked about, constantly evoked, Mr. X becomes established, just as the uncertain place (a country road, somewhere in France perhaps) acquires the feel of a locality, and the timeless time (always, never, fifty years from the turn of the century) is felt as a succession of concrete occasions. At all events, the name of Godot compels something like total allegiance in a situation where nothing has been guaranteed, before and beyond the necessary act of waiting itself.

The emptiness of the situation is not the emptiness of nullity but rather that of a silence which is gradually being filled with sounds, or of a canvas where, with each brushstroke, figures take shape and arrest attention. It is probably true that characters like Estragon and Vladimir could not have found themselves in that kind of denuded space–time before (in *our* sense of space–time), around 1945 and after, somewhere in Western Europe. For it had taken that long for the originally existentialist notion of man 'being thrown into the world' without previous definition, goal or essence, to become not just an idea but a *feeling* – a potentially universal feeling. The two central characters attend to all-important trivia (boots and urination) as they attend to their one life-consuming yet possibly trivial quest; they attend to each other's needs as much as to the terrible demands of the self. And all this attending (a word cognate with waiting, as we can see from the French title and from the connotations of 'waiting on') amounts to lives being lived.

To see the act of waiting as centred, need not lessen our awareness of diminishment. The whole act of waiting takes the form of a cycle run-down (see below, pp. 41–2). We perceive a process of dying, both psychic and physical, in the condition of all four characters. In so far as Estragon and Vladimir can be pictured at all as 'ordinary human beings', they will be pictured as having a great future *behind* them: Estragon may have been a poet, once, but he is now content to quote and adapt (e.g. from Shelley on the moon, 'Pale for weariness', p. 52); Vladimir may have been a thinker, but he can now only reflect on a lyrical fragment thrown out by the rhetorical Pozzo ('Astride of a grave and a difficult birth', pp. 89–90). Their energies, their appetites, are ebbing. The fantasised prospect of an erection – a by-product of hanging – makes Estragon 'highly excited' (stage direction in the uncensored second edition, p. 17). The dread of the night, a nightmare, cannot be shaken off when the day breaks; ailments and fears get worse. It is an early example of Beckett using 'ordinary' images of ageing and impotence as pointers to man's decay. Pozzo and Lucky are, among other things, extreme versions of the frailty of the other couple: Pozzo moving from the peacock-like strutting of a self-assured squire to the blind man calling out for help; Lucky moving from the attempt to rehearse the supreme tenets of an age of faith to the language of broken clichés and metaphysics; after that, the affliction of dumbness is a release. Nature, though not much in the picture, is perhaps running down too; there are no more carrots (only turnips); only the four or five leaves of the solitary tree counteract the bare plain, perhaps to puzzle the voyagers. The human universe is running out of substance, intermittently suggesting a mythic hell in which the fire had died out – a 'void', a 'charnel-house'. But unlike *Endgame* and Beckett's later plays, the play ends with a kind of everlasting beginning.

Confronted with the illusory nature of the waiting, and the certainty (the only certainty) of movement towards extinction, most readers/spectators ask at one point: is this not a mockery of all human effort? The vision of the play is, rather, ambivalent, mixing parody and humour in modern tragicomedy (as the subtitle proclaims). The fluctuations of darkness and light are deliberately unresolved. The images of possible consolation (the tree, 'one of the thieves was saved', the Boy-messenger) are offered, withdrawn, re-offered, questioned, bracketed. Yet they are images which, in our culture, are still charged with emotional power. Even Lucky's breakdown speech throws out highly charged particles of energy, as if through fission: 'loves us dearly with some exceptions for reasons unknown but time will tell'. And the questing characters finally keep faith, having refused to abandon their task, each other, and their own uncertain identity. Vladimir can explicitly boast, with 'billions' of other people (according to Estragon):

We have kept our appointment, and that's an end to that. We are not saints, but we have kept our appointment. How many people can boast as much? (p. 80)

Character and dialogue

When *Waiting for Godot* became famous in the mid-fifties the non-personal or puppet-like abstraction of the paired characters made a particularly strong impact. This was so partly because various types of naturalistic and realistic drama (from Ibsen to Sartre, Miller and others) had accustomed readers and audiences to think of character as fleshed out, round, motivated and changing like a person known in the actual world with whom we could identify, sympathetically or otherwise. This concept of character, though relatively naive, is clear-cut and in many respects natural, and it was certainly widely shared by the reading public and the audiences of the fifties, who were often unfamiliar with non-naturalistic drama: Greek tragedy, the medieval mystery and morality plays as well as modern symbolist drama (late Strindberg, *The Ghost Sonata* and *A Dream Play* and Yeats) and the epic theatre of Brecht. At the same time, the popular theatre – the old melodrama and farce, the music hall and the circus – were hardly considered 'serious'. So strong was the naturalistic concept of character that the stage figures of *Waiting for Godot* tended to be regarded as mere puppets or else as elaborate symbols of split states of mind or as archetypes of measureless significance. What the 'ordinary' theatre-going public lacked in immediate grasp, some of the critics compensated for by speculating endlessly about the origins and philosophical or psychoanalytic implications of Estragon and Vladimir, Pozzo and Lucky. True, their very names bring connotations. The name of Lucky is supremely well chosen for the unfortunate thinker/artist; and Estragon, Vladimir, Pozzo, Lucky (French, Russian, Italian and English names respectively) make up something like a European cross-section. Yet among the most striking features of *Waiting for Godot* is the extent to which Beckett has succeeded in creating a new type of dramatis personae specifically for the theatre, acting like once-popular stage characters. The long introspective monologues of the narrators in

Beckett's fiction (see chapters 8 to 10) give way to embodied figures, both personal and universal, who *interact* with each other, and who have distinct theatrical features: bodies, costumes, gestures, movements, noises, cries, smells and speech styles.

Our reading of the play so far has stressed the way Estragon and Vladimir are both distinct and paired, playing recognisable roles and interacting like persons as well as like actors. Beckett may well have considered the couple a 'pseudocouple' (a term he used for the paired characters of his earlier and unpublished play *Eleutheria*). In the manuscript of *Godot* these two characters do not even have names, but are simply referred to as old men; and when he directed the play, Beckett emphasised similarities of appearance, costume and so on. Indeed it would be a mistake not to perceive an underlying resemblance between the two men, whether the stress is on their age, on their 'trampishness', or on their role as comedians. But it is one thing to see them as 'two of a kind', and another to merge them in some hypothetical entity (as split-off halves of one personality). Even if the view of Estragon and Vladimir as aspects of 'the divided self' were sound, performance brings out the lively personal interaction between these two opposed characters, in a continuous duet.

Let us take a closer look at Estragon and Vladimir as characters, who in turn interact with the other 'pseudocouple', Pozzo and Lucky, as it were doubling their double act.

Each character is distinct, especially in performance. Estragon is far more heart-centred – going through a gamut of emotion from naive hope to black despair, from rebelliousness to childish dependence (Vladimir even has to sing a lullaby for him in Act II), and displaying an inspired clownishness. By contrast, Vladimir is the 'thinker', with all that entails in gestures of detachment, playing the role of the senior partner, the consoler and the reflector on common destiny. Their attitudes clash continuously, so that – working against the stillness and the stasis – much of their enacted relationship is made up of sequences of disagreement and contest, spontaneous or contrived, to kill time. They part and come together in spasms of movement that correspond to failing attempts at separation (a recurrent motif). The lines of their dialogue often converge, like the cross-talk of music-hall performers, yet their speech is often quite idiosyncratic. For example, Vladimir's longer meditative monologues in Act II could not come from Estragon; on the other hand, questions like 'What do we do now?' become part of Estragon's stage-voice, just as much as his oft-repeated and despairing 'Ah' cry (in answer to the non-news about Godot). Cumulatively, these almost-persons and near-characters go on 'making words' together as, in a different kind of play, a couple might make love.

Like many sparring partners – especially in the conventions of comedy and music hall – Estragon and Vladimir are bonded by shared afflictions as well as by affections. They are, strictly speaking, interdependent and twinned; they are compelled to co-operate willy-nilly, and for much of the time they dance the steps of an intimate encounter. We have already seen how much of their act of 'passing the time', proving their existence to each other, is necessarily a double act: their kind of being-in-waiting could *not* become manifest in total isolation, through a string of monologues. The opening scene is, among other things, an act of reunion, gently parodied in Vladimir's ceremonious words: 'Together again at last! We'll have to celebrate this. But how? (*He reflects.*) Get up till I embrace you' – an effusion greeted with an irritable grunt by Estragon: 'Not now, not now.' So the mood is set for countless 'debates' over the second thief, over Godot's status or conditions, the right way to treat Pozzo and Lucky, the way to question the Boy. Even their talk about talking comes in self-conscious yet ultimately 'agreeable' duets:

ESTRAGON: In the meantime let's try and converse calmly, since we're incapable of keeping silent.
VLADIMIR: You're right, we're inexhaustible.   (p.62)

And a longer sequence:

VLADIMIR: When you seek you hear.
ESTRAGON: You do.
VLADIMIR: That prevents you from finding.
ESTRAGON: It does.
ESTRAGON: You think all the same.
VLADIMIR: No, no, impossible.
ESTRAGON: That's the idea, let's contradict each other.
VLADIMIR: Impossible.
ESTRAGON: You think so?
VLADIMIR: We're in no danger of ever thinking any more.
ESTRAGON: Then what are we complaining about?
VLADIMIR: Thinking is not the worst.
ESTRAGON: Perhaps not, but at least there's that.
VLADIMIR: That what?
ESTRAGON: That's the idea, let's ask each other questions.
VLADIMIR: What do you mean at least there's that?

ESTRAGON: That much less misery.
VLADIMIR: True.
ESTRAGON: Well? If we gave thanks for our mercies?　　　　(p.64)

Clearly, this has something of the vigour of spontaneous, colloquial exchanges, though it is stylised within a frame of artifice. In
a series of challenges and responses, expected and unexpected sayings jostle, like Estragon's teasing repartees (from 'You do' to
'That's the idea, let's contradict each other') which cut into and
break up Vladimir's musings on 'thinking'. There are questions
that have the sound of questions calling for an answer; sometimes
there is an answer, and sometimes not, in a controlled randomness, as can be seen from the follow-up from the sequence quoted
above:

ESTRAGON: Well? If we gave thanks for our mercies?
VLADIMIR: What is terrible is to *have* thought.
ESTRAGON: But did that ever happen to us?
VLADIMIR: Where are all these corpses from?

Vladimir's private meditation goes on and cuts across
Estragon's questions. Yet these two remain in a 'satisfactory'
communicative frame, supporting each other's need to talk –
words against the void – whether or not this talk meets the
requirements of what we consider 'good talk', 'co-operative conversation'. The endless verbal inventiveness is flexible enough to
sustain the speakers' endless interest in each other, and the
audience's two-hour interest in their precarious destiny.

Pozzo and Lucky must rank among the few supreme metaphor-
characters in world drama. Each is unique, yet they are inseparable, their master–slave opposition is powerfully enacted on every
level: in their physical appearance, in their voice and speech, and
in the many psychological and social images suggested by their
terrible act. The main image is probably sado-masochistic bondage. All the same, their arrival, and their share of stage time and
space, is perfectly integrated in the action of 'waiting', so that
Pozzo and Lucky interact with Estragon and Vladimir (even
Lucky's long, fragmented thought-tirade is a focus for the other
three, who act as an involved stage audience). Add to this the
overall audio-visual impact of their coming, presence and departure: Pozzo's whip-cracking and shouting followed by his rotund
courtesies of greeting; Lucky entering backwards, his jerky
movements, obeying shouted orders like a circus animal, the shuffling feet, the ceaseless panting, the body trembling under the

weight of basket and baggage, and many other details (the stage directions are as precise as a choreography for dancers). The overall effect may be compared with those scenes in *King Lear* which bring together the mad King and the Fool, flanked by the gibbering, demon-tongued Poor Tom. As drama, it is both timeless and new. Beckett has not drawn on myth or folklore directly, and he has avoided the kind of stage symbol that is rationally explained by the dialogue (like Ibsen's wild duck), which presents an explicit allegorical message. Pozzo and Lucky remain puzzling yet clear, disturbing yet immediate and essentially simple figures.

The fusion of ordinary and extraordinary elements in the characters greatly contributes to this overall impact. Pozzo is both landlord and 'Lord of the Void', a petty but conceited squire (more or less turn-of-the-century, with some Irish overtones, carrying stool, pipe, vaporiser, etc.), gradually heightened to suggest the worst of all tyrants: one who owns the mind of his servile servant and totally dehumanises him. Lucky, by contrast, embodies the image of everybody's 'lost intellectual'. His ruined body and mind also suggest the victim of torture, in a world of asylums and prison camps. Whatever further symbolic action is suggested by the Pozzo and Lucky scenes, this primary level of terror, framed by Pozzo's verbal pomp and circumstance, remains. Pozzo as landlord (claiming ownership of the land Estragon and Vladimir regard as the appointed place for meeting Godot, the Pozzo of Act I), could qualify for a comic character of vanity and pride in a traditional satire. His posture is condescending, his talk inflated, his ideas are made up of social clichés and sentimental windbaggery. The grand seigneur is also the grand spectator gazing at specimens of humanity, at Estragon and Vladimir:

Yes, gentlemen, I cannot go for long without the society of my likes. (*He puts on his glasses and looks at the two likes.*) Even when the likeness is an imperfect one. (*He takes off his glasses.*)

This aspect of the character is then expanded into Pozzo the actor/speech-maker (on the pale and luminous sky, among other topics) craving applause:

How did you find me? Good? Fair? Passable? Mediocre? Positively bad? . . . I have such a need of encouragement! (*Pause.*) I weakened towards the end, you didn't notice? (*Estragon plays up to all this with ironic blarney.*)

The actor is in turn heightened into the impresario or the circus master, who carries a whip, keeps jerking the rope that ties Lucky, and shouts barbaric orders at his creature. It is Lucky ('My Lucky') who had taught him 'all these beautiful things' he speaks of: 'Beauty, grace, truth of the first water.' So Pozzo, the thought-master, is wholly parasitical on Lucky the one-time thinker; it is as if he had siphoned off Lucky's thoughts, and now all that is left are clichés for Pozzo from Lucky's disintegrating mind – a broken language, the broken syntax of thought.

Pozzo's cruelty towards Lucky is sharply emphasised throughout the scene in Act I. He is preparing to get rid of him, after Lucky's life-long service, and he speaks about Lucky in his presence as a type to be exterminated: 'such creatures . . . The best thing would be to kill them.' (p. 32) He dismisses Lucky's weeping as undignified, and, in answer to Vladimir's reproaches, stages – in the full theatrical sense – a *scene* of groaning self-pity: 'I can't bear it . . . any longer . . . the way he goes on . . . you've no idea . . . it's terrible . . . he must go . . . (*he waves his arms*) . . . I'm going mad . . . (*he collapses, his head in his hands*) . . . I can't bear it . . .' Thus attention is re-focused on the master, who is beginning to find the torture he has inflicted on his slave rebounding on himself. When he recovers his complacency, he offers a performance of Lucky's thought – for kicks. This gro-tesque image of refined violence evokes socio-political analogues, whether intended or not. (In the first French edition Pozzo and Lucky are referred to as 'les comiques staliniens'.)

The reappearance of Pozzo in Act II as a blind man, given to desperate utterances on time and destiny, with oracular overtones, comes with the force of a turning-point (as in Greek tragedy). The fact that this sudden transformation has not been prepared for by the preceding action ('One day, is that not enough for you, one day like any other day . . . one day I went blind', p. 89) strengthens the impact of Pozzo's crippled condition. He enters the stage with cries of help (unanswered for long minutes of diversionary play-time), and he leaves it with some of the gestures of a tragic hero (in the speech already quoted): 'They give birth astride of a grave, the light gleams an instant, then it's night once more.' One must suppose that a shift of sympathy takes place here, in any audience watching the transformation of the squire-torturer into the suffer-ing blind man. Whatever one's reservations – remembering the moral evil committed by Pozzo, and aware of the element of pom-pous pastiche in his language – some of the mythic analogues of the blind-seer are bound to be invoked: Oedipus is one. This is not to argue that we experience the kind of compassion and empathy that is aroused by the final wretchedness of a tragic hero such as Oedipus or King Lear. But the play does use some of the resonances of the tragic mode, and the fall of Pozzo is more traditional than the disintegration and dumbness of Lucky.

But there is no need to see in Pozzo cosmic significance, as some critics do. Pozzo's role-playing lyrical rhetoric has a strong local effect, but his sayings, on time and on the pathos of life, need not be regarded as central. Pozzo has not reached some stage 'beyond time'. He may have lost his watch, his halfhunter, in Act I (the beat of the chronometer giving way to the beat of his heart), and he makes despairing pronouncements on measuring time ('the blind have no notion of time'), but he also wants to know where he is (the Board?), what the time is (pp. 85–6) and 'what happened exactly'. In this play Pozzo can no more slip out of the human condition through some loop of time, than any other Beckett character. The end is not yet; and though darkness and affliction create the feeling of an 'infinite now' there is still some *way* to go: 'On!'

Lucky is likely to be the most perplexing character for anyone who sees or reads *Waiting for Godot* for the first time. But his role as dehumanised 'thinker' (artist?) is immediately clear, as in his terrible servility to Pozzo, as we have seen. His great broken 'tirade' *depends* on a certain degree of surface incomprehension for its terrifying impact: it should create terror, if the performance is right. At the same time, the drift of the scattered fragments of his 'great argument' is bound to come across even on first exposure. And one can make out the demented logic of the tirade, without spoiling the power of its chaos. The thought world (the only world) of Lucky has been shattered by meditating on various themes: the diminishing presence of a personal god (no longer feeling, moving, speaking: 'divine apathia, divine athambia, divine aphasia'); the condition and sufferings of man abandoned ('seen to waste and pine, waste and pine'); *in spite of* all our 'improvements', sports, penicillin and the rest, there is continued shrinking ('the skull to shrink and waste'). The design of the speech can, and has been, worked out line-by-line, but probably it is best for each reader/listener to work on the speech individually. We need mention only that the speech does gain a special significance if we recall the characteristic context of the 'Beckett world': the sense of a cosmic run-down, the loss of the human sense of the divine, and the breakdown of language itself, are interlinked. In

41

particular, the language of abstract ideas, of rational theology and the consolations of traditional philosophy, have been ground down and emptied. The rapidly deteriorating control over language is an illness (aphasia) that corresponds to a more general loss of meaning. As the syntax of Lucky's speech deteriorates, it releases – as through fission – repeated little phrases and isolated lyrical words:

> fading, fading, fading . . . on, on . . .
> alas alas   on on
> the skull   the skull   the skull   the skull

until the speech runs down in shouting, repetition and gibberish. The broken speaker has to be forcibly silenced, by seizing his hat. Lucky's tirade is probably remembered by everyone who has heard it as the ultimate exposure of man's fragility – the precariousness of the human voice, of articulate speech, and thought, embodied in the crippled figure who runs down like an over-used automaton.

Theatre and structure

Waiting for Godot has been termed an 'anti-play', in a highly questionable catch-phrase which underlines its reduced 'dramatic' qualities: its lack of plot and logical movement (from exposition through turning-point to catastrophe), its digressions, and so on. Even so, no one has suggested that the scenes of the play should be shuffled, that we should perform it starting from the middle, or the end . . . If such randomness sounds like nonsense, it can at least make us reflect on the play's peculiar tautness of design; how balanced and interlinked are its scenes (and its digressions) along the axis of the two acts, with repetition and variation, and its overall symmetry.

Waiting for Godot uses and parodies what we expect from drama and the theatre, playing on our expectations by changing and counterpointing them. Even the two-act structure, the repetition of two cycles – which a wit called 'nothing happens, twice' – exploits our expectation of a 'dramatic' curve of action, relentless movement towards the final goal – as we know it from realist drama and from several Shakespeare plays.

Much of the tension in waiting (see p. 25 above) comes from audience expectations of a 'dramatic' pattern. The rise/fall is expected and is disappointed, and so is the fall/rise; what we then get is a wholly new pattern, appropriate to a new kind of tragicomedy. The repeated acts also underline the endless action-in-non-action cycles, suggesting an infinite series: the end of the play *could* be the beginning of a third act, leading on to a fourth and fifth act, and so *ad infinitum*. But the economy of the two-act structure does its work well enough – pointing to potential infinity. We might think of Vladimir and Estragon as turning with a revolving stage that brings them back – at the end of each act – to the place they started from. Their space–time is cyclic, and they cannot opt out of their slow revolutions any more than the actor can leave off a role, step off the revolving stage.

The broad scenic units of the play – the two appearances of Pozzo and Lucky (a climax in each act) and of the Boy (a possible turning-point) are so constructed as to underline the repetition. Many other lesser units of construction help to emphasise this circularity, notably Vladimir's round song about the dog at the opening of Act II, which could go on 'for ever'. At the same time, the characters are moving in a definite direction – they are moving onward, or in Pozzo's favourite monosyllable 'On'. Onward looks like downward; their ageing, their deterioration, their time-spinning, are all part of a run-down, towards their eventual end. That sense of time's inexorable movement – onward movement as we know it and fear it, through doing and wasting – is integrated into the cyclic structure. It is made felt through the emphasis on a performance: an occasion here and now that passes the time for the audience, and which must be brought to an end. Internal references to time (the retrospect to the young Estragon and Vladimir, for example, the time, fifty years ago, when they might have jumped off the Eiffel Tower with dignity) further underline our ordinary time-consciousness. The long line of a possible past and a possible future cuts across the rotation of time present, the action before us.

The empty stage itself is clearly a device to magnify theatricality. Beckett does not use the empty stage as fully and elaborately as Pirandello does in *Six Characters in Search of an Author* (1921), to exploit the painful tension between so-called 'illusion' and assumed 'reality'. In *Waiting for Godot* the main function of staging the stage itself, as the setting of the action, is to underline its emptiness – a space to be filled with words and images (a tree, the moon rising at the end of Act I). Nothing quite like that has ever been attempted, though neither Greek nor Elizabethan drama relied on stage props, and modern stage design (from Craig and Appia on) has increasingly used the stage as an 'empty space', for reconstructing space. Drawing attention to the stage has the further benefit of distancing the action from the audience and pointing to players, roles, contrived movements, speech-making, the perpetual rehearsal of an improvised text that gets fixed. Imagination creates everything 'out of airy *nothing*'. Jokes and jocular allusions keep the physical 'obviousness' of the stage continuously before the audience, starting from the quietly ironic insult to the public:

Estragon moves to the centre, halts with his back to auditorium.
ESTRAGON: Charming spot. (*He turns, advances to front, halts facing auditorium.*)
  Inspiring prospects. (*He turns to Vladimir.*) Let's go. (p. 13)

In the middle of the first Pozzo and Lucky episode, just at the point where Pozzo is speaking in his most histrionic manner, like a ham actor, Vladimir and Estragon as stage audience 'let on' that they are aware of the kind of spectacle they have been exposed to and trapped in:

VLADIMIR: Charming evening we're having.
ESTRAGON: Unforgettable.
VLADIMIR: And it's not over.
ESTRAGON: Apparently not.
VLADIMIR: It's only beginning.
ESTRAGON: It's awful.
VLADIMIR: Worse than pantomime.
ESTRAGON: The circus.
VLADIMIR: The music hall.
ESTRAGON: The circus. (p. 35)

The irony of this internal reference to 'what is going on here in the theatre' gives the audience the chance to reflect on its own 'charming evening', and the attendant risks of 'it' not yet being over, as the digressions multiply. The reference to pantomime (the French version has *spectacle*), music hall and circus, sharpens awareness of the circus clown antics of Vladimir and Estragon (whether or not performed on a circus-like stage, as it was at the Round House, in 1981), and the music-hall patter in their dialogue can be distinctly heard.

The inward-pointing theatre metaphors are intensified in Act II where the enclosed but 'spacious' space of the theatre is used as an analogy for a place without exit, hell. In a triumphant moment the sounds heard off-stage are taken to announce the coming of Godot 'at last': Vladimir calls out to Estragon and drags him towards the wings, on the right, but Estragon 'gets lost' through his exit; Vladimir runs to meet him on the extreme left, but Estragon re-enters on the right. It is then that he cries out 'I'm in hell', in a context that makes it clear that all the exits have been blocked:

VLADIMIR: We're surrounded! (*Estragon makes a rush towards back.*) Imbecile! There's no way out there. (*He takes Estragon by the arm and drags him towards front.*) There! Not a soul in sight! Off you go. Quick! (*He pushes Estragon towards auditorium. Estragon recoils in horror.*) You won't? (*He contemplates auditorium.*) Well, I can understand that. Wait till I see. (*He reflects.*) Your only hope left is to disappear. (p. 74)

The analogy, between the panic-stricken person who does not know which way to turn in an all-enveloping 'hell' and the actor suffering from stage fright (wanting to use the back as exit, and the front too), is one of many fused tragicomic effects. The music-hall-type joke of commenting on the auditorium does not lessen the horror. The audience is supposed to be absent, yet, presumably, it is the thought of facing the audience that adds to Estragon's horror when facing the auditorium – a double theatrical joke.

Such overt pointers to the theatre are reinforced by the most visible kind of physical stage routines: the boot-games, the long hat-passing number, the conscious miming, play-acting and cursing, which have been summarised earlier in this chapter. These are the acts that owe most to the popular theatre, especially to the English music hall, and the double act of vaudeville ('Flanagan and Allen'), though Beckett was doubtless also influenced by the comedians of the silent film (especially Chaplin and Buster Keaton) and perhaps also by Laurel and Hardy. The source matters much less than the revitalised use of elements of farce and clowning in the serious theatre.

The 'tragicomedy' is so pervasive that it probably covers all the scenes of the play. The two failed suicide attempts are memorable examples, especially the second one ('You could hang on to my legs.' / 'And who'd hang on to mine?'), placed precariously near the end of the play; but it is carefully timed to sustain the 'tragicomic tone' right to the end. The Pozzo and Lucky scenes fuse not just the tragic and the comic, but also the melodramatic and the farcical, in rapidly shifting tones. The episode in Act II where Pozzo goes on shouting for help while Estragon and Vladimir ignore or debate the situation risks broad farce – with the cumulative falls, and the sporting commentary on who is up,

who down – in a scene that must accommodate the tragic overtones of Pozzo's blindness and his despairing speech on time and
universal darkness. Similarly, the violence of Lucky's role – the
kicks and counter-kicks, the terror of his physical and spiritual
enslavement, aphasia and breakdown of thought – are seamlessly
integrated in a circus act, which ends with the seizing of that failed
performer's hat. In Shakespeare there is either comic relief – the
'Hell-Porter' in *Macbeth* – or the comic release that comes from
a happy ending in a potentially tragic pattern (*Measure for Measure*
and *The Winter's Tale*). In Chekhov the causes of laughter and
tears co-exist in a social and personal reality where collisions of
the noble and the banal, of sudden death and creaking boots, are
inevitable. By contrast, *Waiting for Godot* is tragicomic at every
level, from the beginning to the end of the play; from first meeting
to the final failed suicide attempt.

Finding the vision of the play in overall structure and theatricality is not to forget that Beckett is, above all, a master of words.
But the language of *Waiting for Godot* probably makes more allusions to the theatre than any other Beckett play. The characters
often interact through speech as their dialogue is counterpointed
by movement, gesture, auditive and visual effects. It remains true
that Beckett's verbal art springs from an extreme view of
language: a severance of words from objects, a denial that
language can either represent or express the world 'out there',
coupled with a recurrent, hypnotic desire for words to cease – for
silence. *Waiting for Godot* is a fully embodied play *despite* Beckett's
known views on the failure of language, and the total isolation of
the speaker, the human animal that secretes words. The total
impact of the play is richer, more concrete and multi-vocal than
might be expected from Beckett's virtual negation of art and
language. As our reading has tried to show, Beckett's dramatic
and verbal art embodies precise images of action and a far-
reaching vision of human existence. The impact of the play has
not weakened in over three decades and is likely to endure, as far
as a contemporary can tell, for all time.

3

Endgame

Beckett has inherited the modernist writer's creed of 'making it new'. Each new work must be an innovation not only in relation to all known forms of literature and drama, but also in relation to the author's previous work. So *Endgame* can be seen as a wholly new kind of play while, at the same time, it also carries certain aspects of *Waiting for Godot* to further points of intensity and compression. It is as if Beckett had been dissatisfied with the well-tempered tragicomedy in *Waiting for Godot*, which left that play open to semi-naturalistic, humanist or life-affirming productions (as in the first London production in 1955). He wanted to distil a darker vision, 'more inhuman than Godot',[1] in a one-act structure that gradually closes in like the final scene of a traditional tragedy. The open road of *Godot* is replaced by a prison-cell-like room that has two tiny windows with views of an almost dead universe. The relatively mobile Estragon and Vladimir give way to a couple whose mobility is limited in the extreme: Hamm, pushed in his chair, can only hug the walls of his minuscule stage-kingdom; and Clov, who cannot sit, can only run to and fro from wall to wall, from centre to circumference. In Beckett's most famous stage image, Nell and Nagg spend the entire 'action' confined to dustbins – legless, in perfect immobility. The cyclic run-down and the exhaustion of all physical and psychic resources is intensified; the cycle is not repeated and the ending has a starker finality. (The detail is complex, as we shall see, but this is the broad pattern.) The metaphysics of the play is also chillier, with more ruthless glimpses of 'nothingness' beyond the surface puppetry; there are scenes that explicitly parody worship, love and the residual quest for meaning. Finally, the dialogue too is pared down to stark simplicity, in places to a minimal vocabulary. If the text is still found difficult on first encounter, that is due to its compression: with static devices which suggest that the needle has got stuck. But it is a text that many readers and audiences have found moving – it does 'claw', to use Beckett's word about the play – and if solitary reading enhances the bleakness of its spiritual landscape, a public performance evokes frequent and sympathetic laughter.

47

'Nearly finished'

To begin a play with the word 'finished' is in itself a unique opening in world drama. To embody 'ending' as a process, at every level of action (character and language, vision and structure), might be thought to contradict all the known elements of traditional drama. Yet 'ending' is as much the stuff of this play as 'waiting' is of the earlier play – a theatre metaphor that is not just evoked but consistently enacted. The play exploits the manifold and overlapping connotations the idea of *ending* has for us – completing a set, a game of chess, a story, a performance; ending a relationship, parting; ending a life, preparing to die; end of the world, last things, apocalypse – with relentless concentration. Not since the morality plays of the late Middle Ages has drama been so saturated with universal-seeming symbols; yet the play has no 'programme', no allegorical or didactic purpose, and cannot be interpreted (despite all the critical efforts) definitively. The experience of the play seems to imitate its central metaphor – the ending is an endless process.

The opening words of Clov repeat: 'nearly finished, it must be nearly finished'. That is, reader and audience are immediately located at some point of crisis – comparable to the final stage of an illness, the last scene of a play, or the curve that tantalisingly, almost-but-never-quite, reaches a straight line. We are introduced to a slow, painful, drop-by-drop ('grain upon grain') process. Hamm sitting motionless in his chair, as if stricken, embodies from the start the sense of an ending, both physically and metaphorically. Hamm is, among other things, the perpetual invalid, perhaps with a touch of hypochondria or at least a fine sense of self-dramatised suffering: handkerchief spread out before him, wiping his eyes, clearing his throat. His tone mocks the cadences of high tragedy (as we shall see): 'Can there be misery – (*he yawns*) – loftier than mine? No doubt. Formerly. But now?' This victim of debility seems strong enough to have mastery; drifting towards extinction, he appears to have a choice, more like a man rehearsing death or contemplating suicide than a man lying on his deathbed, not to be resuscitated. Hamm soliloquises:

Enough, it's time it ended, in the refuge too. (*Pause.*) And yet – And yet I hesitate, I hesitate to . . . to end. Yes, there it is, it's time it ended and yet I hesitate to – (*he yawns*) – to end. (*Yawns.*)

Hamm has now struck one of his keynotes, a double note that introduces both the role-acting sick man of comedy and the dying king of tragedy. Each note is often heard, fluctuating or converging, throughout the play. The grand monologues of the tired monarch are further interwoven with attempts at fatherly conversation with Clov, the servant-son, on topics that include the problem of Clov leaving and the action ending. Occasionally, a remark is thrown at the decrepit parents in their dustbins, or Hamm makes a gesture to the universe or towards the audience (see pp. 61–6 for details). Meanwhile, he spends most of his left-over time on little circular journeys that explore what is left of his diminishing space, the cell-like room. Beyond that, he contents himself with reports of a dying universe and self-conscious rehearsals of his last story and of his final soliloquy.

Let us see how this pattern of ending is worked out, with its own dramatic tension that counteracts inertia: Hamm's bursts of energy pushing against his yawning boredom. The initial attempt at refusing the new day altogether ('Get me ready, I'm going to bed', p. 13), gives way to quite a brisk way of ordering time – by giving orders to Clov, for example: 'Get me ready. (*Clov does not move.*) Go and get the sheet. (*Clov does not move.*) Clov!' Giving orders, like asserting his superiority through oaths, is one source of energy for Hamm in attempting to get through the day. Even so, within minutes of acting time, weariness and pain are re-asserted: 'This is slow work. (*Pause.*) Is it not time for my pain-killer?' (p. 16); then the day that had hardly begun is referred to as 'the end of the day' (p. 17). After the sustained interlude of Nell and Nagg's duet (to which Hamm listens, mostly as a motionless spectator), Hamm initiates what looks like the principal ritual of the day: the journey round the room, 'right round the world!' (pp. 23–6). In a series of superbly placed and repeated orders, Hamm insists on being pushed to the centre – 'right in the centre', 'bang in the centre' – of his shrunken kingdom. The postures of 'I'm a monarch of all I survey' have never been as economically dramatised, for the craving for power and knowledge are exactly matched by images of Hamm's almost total impotence. (Those who know Ionesco's *Exit the King* (1962), may contrast Beckett's handling of the single scene with Ionesco's play, which dwells on the theme of dying for two hours.) As if to compensate for the dissatisfactions of the room, the confined space within the blank walls, Hamm orders Clov to inspect the universe, through the windows, with the help of a telescope. Clov reports a zero vision, a 'corpsed' external world, waves like lead, grey light from pole to pole.

This central ritual gives way to a series of lesser ones, which parody the slow ending of time: the hunting of the last flea, Hamm's prophecy of an empty apocalypse (p. 28), of a place where even Clov must come to a standstill (p. 29), and Hamm's growing desire for extinction ('Why don't you finish us', p. 29). This death-wish is echoed by the allusive use of the word 'extinguished' (alluding to a fragment from one of Hamm's stories, the death of Mother Pegg and her light). When his chair is immobilised, Hamm tells the story of the madman who thought the end of the world had come – another Chinese-box effect, end-story within end-story. The farcical ringing of the alarm clock seems to mock the tolling of bells for doomsday ('Fit to wake the dead'), and Hamm's first long story (whose brief prologue repeats Clov's opening lines, 'finished, we're finished') relates how 'the sun went down among the dead' (p. 36). When that story is nearly finished, and Nell fails to answer Nagg's call, Hamm solemnly announces 'Our revels here are ended.'

The quotation (Prospero's words from Act IV of *The Tempest*) marks the place for a formal ending; more correctly, a series of endings or half-endings that keep groping towards yet another, more final-seeming, finale. Hamm is drained from the prolonged creative effort (his story), there is no more tide, and Nell is coldly pronounced dead. By now the making of an end is palpable: the play is grinding to a halt, as the cliché has it, through built-in stalling devices. In his second 'me to play' soliloquy Hamm voices his most significant recognition: 'The end is in the beginning and yet you go on. (*Pause.*) Perhaps I could go on with my story, end it and begin another' (pp. 44–5). These two sentences juxtapose, and imaginatively fuse, two kinds of 'endless ending' – living *and* writing. The actual ending of the play rehearses certain elements from a traditional tragedy (see pp. 61–3); Hamm's melodramatic wish to be killed by Clov ('hit me with the gaff', 'Put me in my coffin') and what sounds like his cosmic death-wish: 'Then let it end! . . . with a bang!' (p. 49). After that there remains only the playing out of the ceremony of Clov's departure and Hamm's third 'me to play' soliloquy, enacting a ritual of self-abdication with gestures 'to end up with' – discarding the dog and the whistle, and refolding the blood-stained handkerchief over his face. Thus the much-rehearsed and serene ending echoes the beginning – a deliberately theatrical tableau, with a prolonged silence before the curtain falls on the motionless draped figure of Hamm.

Hamm's own process of 'ending' is inseparably linked to other kinds of ending, embodied in the action and in several types of apocalyptic imagery. The coming of the end is experienced on several planes:

1. Physical decay – the end of things, persons, creatures and creature comforts of every kind. 'No more' is a key phrase in the text: no more bicycle wheels, no more pap, no more sugar-plums, no more Turkish delight, no more rugs, no more pain-killer (only pain as a killer) and, towards the end, no more coffins. A gradual yet finally total exhaustion of all resources accompanies the last state of man, the last state of Hamm anyway.

The characters (or dramatic figures) exhibit the usual Beckettian symptoms of physical degeneration. Hamm is probably paralysed; and he suffers from other barely diagnosable symptoms, like some kind of bleeding ('ever since fontanelle'). Nell dies in her dustbin and Nagg is silenced. Before their end, the parents enact the final stages of their grotesque yet pathos-filled decrepitude. At one point Nagg says to Nell, who has no legs, no sight, no hearing:

NAGG: Our hearing hasn't failed.
NELL: Our what?
NAGG: Our hearing. (p. 18)

Nagg and Nell cannot kiss across their separate bins, and their physical impotence has its counterpart in the loss of feeling, in Clov's inability to love:

HAMM: You don't love me.
CLOV: No.
HAMM: You loved me once.
CLOV: Once! (p. 14)

Later on, in Hamm's play-speech, love is explicitly mocked: 'Get out of here and love one another. Lick your neighbour as yourself' (p. 44). And love is tonelessly lamented by the departing Clov in the final sequence: 'They said to me, That's love, yes, yes, not a doubt, now you see how – ' (p. 50).

Something like a cosmic curse has entered the created world; Hamm (like Lear) curses procreation, calls his father 'accursed progenitor' and 'accursed fornicator' (pp. 15, 16). The possibility of any form of new life is met with terror: a flea, or a rat, and, of course, a child, threaten to start the whole process of life again. So they must be exterminated. The sighting of a young boy near the end (an episode deliberately reduced by Beckett) brings the threat of a 'potential procreator', together with the fear that there can be no *end* . . . (pp. 49–50).

2. Beyond the human ending, the whole of Nature is ending – the elements, space, time, the cosmos perhaps.

HAMM: Nature has forgotten us.
CLOV: There's no more nature.
HAMM: No more nature! You exaggerate.
CLOV: In the vicinity. (p. 116)

From the window-like slits within, all the readings out there are ZERO: no earth, no sea, the light is sunk (pp. 24–5). More precisely, the light is grey (as it is in *Malone Dies*). In Clov's totalitarian vision all is 'corpsed' (p. 25); and 'The whole place stinks of corpses' (p. 33). However, there is still a degree of openness or uncertainty about some of the apocalyptic prospects. For instance, there is the madman in Hamm's story who could see nothing in the beauty of the world except ashes? ('All that rising corn! And there! Look. The sails of the herring fleet!', p. 32.) It is not clear whether Hamm's vision is identical with that of the madman who thought that the end of the world had come. The uncertainty allows the evocation of images of creation and fertility (rising corn) as earlier on Hamm evoked, with ironic nostalgia, the classical goddesses of Nature: 'Flora! Pomona! (*Ecstatically*) Ceres!' (p. 30). Again, when Hamm recites to Clov a hypnotic tirade on the terror of the last things ('infinite emptiness will be all around you, all the resurrected dead of all the ages wouldn't fill it . . .'), Clov answers quietly, after a pause: 'It's not certain' (pp. 28–9).

3. The end of the body and the end of Nature are accompanied, as well they might be, by the end of all existential and metaphysical comforts: the end of meaning, the death of God; the end of time.

HAMM: We're not beginning to . . . to . . . mean something?
CLOV: Mean something! You and I, mean something! (*Brief laugh.*) Ah that's a good one! (p. 27)

HAMM: (*Whose prayer has not been answered*): The bastard! He doesn't exist!
CLOV: Not yet. (p. 38)

HAMM: Moments for nothing, now as always, time was never and time is over . . . (p. 52)

The fusion of all these planes of ending – lives, the planet, the universe – cumulatively suggests that *Endgame* is, among other things, a kind of black creation story – that is, a parable of creation in reverse, non-generation. But it would be a mistake to see the play as a tight modern allegory, a systematic negative version of, say, Dante's vision of hell in *The Divine Comedy*. Rather, we are dealing with a play that exploits the seemingly anti-dramatic process of 'making an end' in such a total way that on almost every page of the text an image of 'ending' is evoked. Among all the images mentioned so far, the image suggested by the title, a game of chess, might well appear to be the weakest, for we are left with the mere suggestion of final movements – the king being taken relentlessly, step-by-step, to checkmate. In terms of action, and even in terms of imagery, the chess analogy does not work concretely or with any particular force.

The metaphor of cosmic extinction probably finds a response in a great number of people; it is perfectly possible that as human beings we have a collective sense of the world's end – it can enter our dreams and fantasies, and it is certainly part of many great myths (the Babylonian Gilgamesh, the Biblical Flood, the Scandinavian Ragnarok). Those looking for more immediate contexts will point to the fear of annihilation in a nuclear war, a fear that first spread in Europe in the fifties. And beyond that precise catastrophe, there is modern man's consciousness – in keeping with the second law of thermodynamics, the law of entropy – that the universe as we know it is gradually running down or levelling out its sources of energy. A response to *Endgame* does not require such specific contexts, though certain parallels – mythic, H-bomb-conscious, scientific – may predispose us to respond to the action and imagery of the play. As in the play, so in our experience of it, the permutations of ending seem endless.

Character and dialogue

The four characters of *Endgame* are even more highly stylised – in terms of role, speech, physical appearance and movement – than are the characters of *Waiting for Godot*. Yet Hamm and Clov, and, to a lesser extent, Nagg and Nell, develop into distinct figures who interact in significant and memorable ways. The general argument concerning Beckett's first 'pseudocouple' (see chapter 2, p. 36) applies to *Endgame* as well: it is not helpful to regard the characters as mere abstractions, allegorical personifications that can be exhaustively interpreted if only we can find the key to their meaning. The relationships established, by the action and dialogue, seem to offer the best starting points for any precise discussion of these characters, leaving until later their roles and significance in and beyond the play.

A love–hate relationship, with hints of a long past of conflicts and emotions, is established between Hamm and Clov from the start, and sustained through their duologues. All of these are poignantly personal and immediate, involving such clear physical/spiritual acts as caring for and challenging each other, and preparing for the end of their relationship (Clov leaving Hamm). The peculiar intimacy of the relationship stands out against frequent parodies of tenderness and love in the dialogue. The interaction of Hamm and Clov remains coherent, even though much remains tentative – uncertainties and half-clues abound. Finally, we witness certain points of convergence between the speakers while they remain sharply, even grotesquely, contrasted in physical appearance, a constant visual counterpoint in performance. Hamm cannot stand up, Clov cannot sit down; Hamm is bulky and tends to heavy tragic acting (the ham actor), while Clov is slender and subtle-seeming, and tends to look and act like a clown. One of the unforgettable sound effects of the play is the light patter of footsteps across the stage accompanying a patter of phrases as Clov runs errands for his imperious master. (The only physical feature they have in common is the stylised red face, a feature in the stage directions which Beckett dropped when co-directing the play.)

The opening exchanges between Hamm and Clov (pp. 13–18) present several of the key features of this intimate relationship. Clov is shown as Hamm's attendant (as it were covering a spectrum from nurse to servant), comparable to Lucky in this respect, but far less abject and fully articulate. Their ambivalent love–hate relationship, veering from tenderness to sadism, is also established early in the play.

HAMM: Did you ever see my eyes?
CLOV: Pulling back the lids? (*Pause.*) No.
HAMM: One of these days I'll show them you. (*Pause.*) It seems they've
      gone all white. (p. 13)

And a little further on:

CLOV: Why do you keep me?
HAMM: There's no one else.

CLOV: There's nowhere else.
                    Pause.
HAMM: You're leaving me all the same.
CLOV: I'm trying.
HAMM: You don't love me.
CLOV: No.
HAMM: You loved me once.
CLOV: Once!
HAMM: I've made you suffer too much. (*Pause.*) Haven't I?
CLOV: It's not that.
HAMM: (*shocked*). I haven't made you suffer too much?
CLOV: Yes!
HAMM: (*relieved*). Ah you gave me a fright!   (p. 14)

Hamm's punch-line (one of many) is the kind of cruel personal joke that is possible only in intimate dialogue. The motif of parting, which has now been introduced, has the tone of a close couple about it. At all events, the pointers to past love, and past suffering, briefly conjure up an 'endless' relationship, now turned sour, static and precarious, trying but failing to come to a terminal end – like everything else in the play. Most readers and audiences are likely to assume a father–son relationship from this point on, even though the text at no point confirms this (there is a later hint that Clov is an adopted son). The suffering evoked is not made concrete, it is to be seen as inherent in the relationship (all intimate relationship?) and so is the erosion of love, filial, paternal or otherwise.

The black humour mocks the absence of love, but at the same time underpins the couple's inseparability, as in the exchange that always evokes laughter in performance:

HAMM: Why don't you kill me?
CLOV: I don't know the combination of the larder.
                    Pause.
HAMM: Go and get two bicycle wheels.
CLOV: I never had a bicycle.
HAMM: The thing is impossible.
CLOV: When there were still bicycles I wept to have one. I crawled at
          your feet. You told me to get out to hell. Now there are none.
                                                    (p. 15)

The juxtaposition of ordinary 'family conversation' and suicidal or homicidal thoughts in an extreme situation is in itself funny. It suggests the compulsive repetition or rehearsal of past sayings – reproaches, nostalgias – unto the last: this talk may be taking place in the final refuge, but there is time enough, as in *Godot*, for recalling trivial/important incidents from the past, the accumulated psychopathology of everyday lives. (In addition, bicycles are obsessively significant objects for Beckett – as in *Molloy* – mechanical, and tending to fall apart, like mind and body.) The gestures and tones of intimate bickering also pervade those exchanges that have distinct biblical and apocalyptic overtones, the sense of doomsday, as in the allusion to 'the writing on the wall' at Belshazzar's feast: 'mene, mene' ('God hath numbered thy kingdom, and finished it'):

CLOV: I'll leave you, I have things to do.
HAMM: In your kitchen?
CLOV: Yes.
HAMM: What, I'd like to know.
CLOV: I look at the wall.
HAMM: The wall! And what do you see on your wall?
      Mene, mene? Naked bodies?
CLOV: I see my light dying.
HAMM: Your light dying! Listen to that! Well, it can die just as well here, *your* light.
           Pause.
CLOV: You shouldn't speak to me like that.
           Pause.
HAMM: (*coldly*). Forgive me. (*Pause. Louder.*) I said, Forgive me.
CLOV: I heard you. (p. 17)

This well-marked alternation of the familial and the cosmic, along with the familiar and the sublime speech styles, is later intensified to express one of the play's long-echoing questions, in the central episode where Hamm surveys his 'kingdom':

HAMM: Clov!
CLOV: (*impatiently*). What is it?
HAMM: We're not beginning to . . . to . . . mean something?
CLOV: Mean something! You and I, mean something! (*Brief laugh.*) Ah that's a good one!
HAMM: I wonder. (*Pause.*) Imagine if a rational being came back to earth, wouldn't he be liable to get ideas into his head if he observed us long enough. (pp. 26–7)

The ironic tone keeps one of the play's main metaphysical questions open-ended and grounded in personal relationship ('You and I, mean something!'): sufficiently conversational to be compared, on one level, with the banal yet solemn philosophising of characters in a Chekhov play. The question of meaning is not answered, is never answered either in the local dialogue or in terms of the action. For the rest of the play the strands of the personal ending (Clov to leave Hamm) and of the cosmic catastrophe continue to be seamlessly woven together, like a double plot in traditional plays (see pp. 64–5). Thus, one of the characteristic contests between Hamm and Clov (where Hamm torments Clov with a rapid succession of futile demands, p. 28) leads straight to Hamm's dark prophecy: 'One day you'll be blind, like me. (*Pause.*) One day you'll say to yourself, I'm tired, I'll sit down, and you'll go and sit down.' The repeated 'you' address personalises the prophecy, that is, Hamm wishing a kind of everlasting curse on Clov, out of spite, as if motivated by the anger of despised love. Yet, at the same time, we distinctly hear in that speech the voice of some revelation: 'Infinite emptiness will be all around you, all the resurrected dead of all the ages wouldn't fill it, and there you'll be like a little bit of grit in the middle of the steppe.' The speech is also reminiscent of a certain type of hell-fire sermon; the temperature rises but is immediately cooled by Clov's debunking objection to the opening premise of Hamm's prophecy ('and you'll go and sit down'): 'I can't sit down.' The fluctuation of tension is, here and elsewhere, a device that fills the stage with the illusion of constant dramatic action – again as in *Godot*.

The rituals of parting (Clov leaving) keep being repeated, but each is like a rehearsed ceremony, acted out to lessen the distance between time present and the ending of the relationship, which is both dreaded and desired:

CLOV: So you all want me to leave you.
HAMM: Naturally.
CLOV: Then I'll leave you.
HAMM: You can't leave us.
CLOV: Then I shan't leave you.
                    Pause.
HAMM: Why don't you finish us? (*Pause.*) I'll tell you the combination
        of the larder if you promise to finish me.   (p. 29)

In the exchange just quoted the extreme formality of the proceedings is underlined by the plural pronoun – the royal 'us', which ties up with Hamm's role-playing king-act. It also suggests a kind of frozen tableau, like the sculptured events on Keats's Grecian Urn. The immobility of these proceedings – the paradox of movement without motion – is directly exemplified in a later exchange:

HAMM: I can't leave you.
CLOV: I know. And you can't follow me.
Pause.
HAMM: If you leave me how shall I know?
CLOV: (*briskly*). Well you simply whistle me and if I don't come running
it means I've left you.   (p. 33)

The ritual of ending the relationship is further parodied by the alarm-clock episode, in which Clov works out that ingenious signalling device: 'You whistle me. I don't come. The alarm rings. I'm gone. It doesn't ring. I'm dead.' The alarm is duly tried out and Clov, holding it against Hamm's ear, gives his judicious verdict: 'The end is terrific.'

The endless-seeming rituals of the final phase, from 'Our revels here are ended' (p. 39), keep repeating the gestures, phrases, and emotional tones of a long but inconclusive farewell. The suggestion of ceremony – and its parody – can hardly be avoided in performance. We might tire of these 'variations on the theme', but text and performance usually succeed in getting across the comic pathos of leaving/not leaving. In a final rebellion, Clov questions the reason for his own obedience ('Perhaps it's compassion', says Hamm), hits the master with his toy dog, implores him to stop *playing*, and announces, with finality – which generates uncertainty – that he is leaving. But before he leaves he is ordered to make a speech, as Lucky was ordered to speak by Pozzo; unlike Lucky's speech, this one is articulate and resonant with the echoes of the whole play, in part a meditation ('What skilled attention they get, all these dying of their wounds'), in part a lament for his own way of leaving ('I open the door of the cell and go. I am so bowed I only see my feet, if I open my eyes, and between my legs a little trail of black dust'). But it is not the 'character', the departing son, who has the last word, but the role-player, the clown: 'this is what we call making an exit', Clov says flatly.

Proper attention to the dialogue of Hamm and Clov makes us see the poignancy of their personal interaction, in an 'as if' father–son relationship. There are aspects of sharp hostility in this relationship, which are also present in the exchanges of Hamm and his father, Nagg – extending the paternal curse across three generations, as if there were a curse on the act of generating life itself.

This aspect of the play can also be seen as a saga of generations, with the focus not on continuity and change but on the general 'mistake' of begetting, being born, and wishing for posterity. We have a compressed and degenerate biblical genealogy: Nagg begat Hamm who begat (probably adopted) Clove who will beget no one, if the scheme of dying Nature is to be fulfilled. In this context the father–son relationship is seen as one of dominant hostility and the cursing of Nagg by Hamm takes on a stronger significance of desired sterility: 'accursed progenitor' and 'accursed fornicator!' Even more explicit is the black comic exchange:

HAMM: Scoundrel! Why did you engender me?
NAGG: I didn't know.
HAMM: What? What didn't you know?
NAGG: That it'd be you.   (p. 35)

This wish to be unborn clearly echoes the wish of Job, and of certain protagonists of traditional tragedy, in climactic moments of suffering. But for Hamm it seems to be a constant wish, governing his will to end 'the game'. The crippled, legless state of Nagg and Nell is itself a parody of the parental couple, emphasised by their attempts at erotic tenderness and by their nostalgia for having once rowed on Lake Como, one April afternoon, the day after they had got engaged (p. 21). (In the first draft typescript of the play Beckett included a black joke on how the couple's accident had made the father impotent, fortunately the day after the nuptials.) Nagg, as father, has nothing of Hamm's ferocious temper; on the contrary, he is given 'paternal love' speeches, made ambivalent through his dependence on his son, having to plead for food and favours (sugar-plums): 'After all I'm your father. It's true if it hadn't been me it would have been someone else' . . . 'I hope the day will come when you'll really need to have me listen to you, and need to hear my voice, any voice. (*Pause.*) Yes, I hope I'll live till then, to hear you calling me like when you were a tiny boy, and were frightened, in the dark, and I was your only hope' (p. 38). This amounts to wishing infantilism on Hamm, at least a better state than the hell Hamm prophesies for Clov! That image of the frightened, helpless, vulnerable child recurs also in the dialogue of Hamm and Clov, when Hamm plays his own father motif, so to speak:

HAMM: Do you remember when you came here?
CLOV: No. Too small, you told me.
HAMM: Do you remember your father?

           . . .

HAMM: It was I was a father to you.

59

CLOV: Yes. (*He looks at Hamm fixedly.*) You were that to me.
HAMM: My house a home for you.
CLOV: Yes. (*He looks about him.*) This was that to me.
HAMM: (*proudly*). But for me (*gesture towards himself*) no father. But for
    Hamm (*gesture towards surroundings*) no home.   (p. 29)

The marked theatricality, broadly hammed gestures and stiff formalities of phrasing, point to a ritual of adoption. The 'as if' son is to act as a real son, that is out of filial gratitude. But that is impossible, for, as we have seen, the whole relationship is out of true, warped by authoritarian father–son games. The patterns of adoption and rejection are mirrored also in one of Hamm's recurrent stories: in the monologue story of the father who had come crawling, on his belly, to beg for bread and then for refuge for his son (pp. 35–7). The 'I'-narrator of the story – who sounds very much like Hamm – appears to reject this act of mercy with tyrannical glee. However, the outcome is uncertain; the child, 'the brat', 'the little boy' is reintroduced in Hamm's second, dialogue version of the story (pp. 40–1) where Hamm and Clov speculate about what the boy *would have done* (climb trees, do little odd jobs) if given refuge. And there is the fleeting apparition of a small boy, glimpsed by Clov in the final movement of the play – 'a potential procreator' – who is condemned to death by the conditions 'out there' (and by the conditions of the text that is ending). We need not think of the returning child as some kind of divine child who might bring partial redemption to a dying world; rather the child seems to embody the innocent sufferer who brings more suffering into the world – as a potential procreator, perpetuator of the endless cycle.

The curse of generation appears to be lifted only in the final movement of the play which has several echoes of a traditional reconciliation or atonement. We may include in the tones of reconciliation the mellowing of Hamm, who sees himself as a solitary being, separated from both father and son: 'I'll have called my father and I'll have called my . . . (*he hesitates*) . . . my son [. . .] Then babble, babble, words, like the solitary child who turns himself into children, two, three, so as to be together, and whisper together, in the dark' (p. 45). These lyrical images appear to reconcile Hamm to the state of his own 'generated' state, but only on the threshold of his father's death and his son's departure. In his solitude it is the inner world of thoughts that 'generates' children; and for the isolated thinker the whole I–you, father–son drama is itself spun out of the 'babble' of solitude.

In his final monologue Hamm twice calls out 'Father' – a call that in our culture carries echoes of the Crucifixion. At the same time it is a call that seems to point back to the significant variations of the father–son relationship across the whole play. What was dramatised as a kind of 'necessary suffering', a created state condemned to issue in life-long bickering and endless efforts of separation, is finally given the dignity of a suffering person's cry.

Theatre and structure

The structure of action in *Endgame* may well seem diminished from the point of view of traditional drama, but the whole play is conceived in thoroughly theatrical terms. The less 'dramatic', the more performance-ready: this paradox springs from the highly play-conscious nature of Beckett's art. Certain theatrical conventions – those of tragedy in particular – are echoed or parodied. The themes of 'playing' and 'ending' are fully embodied in the cyclic structure of the play. The stage and its conditions are 'advertised' along with broad role-playing (Hamm) and play-within-the-play devices. Visual and sound effects are woven into the verbal text in every scene.

It might be said that *Endgame* stages 'all the world' – as did certain kinds of allegorical drama, like Calderón's *The Great Theatre of the World* (1645), but here all is diminished, the characters in number and scope, the action to a slow cycle of ending, the world itself appoaching zero point. Although Beckett avoids explicit allegory, the audience is likely to respond to a human and natural catastrophe being performed on stage, with the king and his fool at the centre. From the long silence and ritual opening of Hamm's brief day to the closing ritual – when Hamm casts off his stage props – episode after episode enacts a 'piece of theatre' and contributes to the total effect of theatricality.

To the present writer the overall effect of *Endgame* suggests the performance of a compressed tragedy or, more precisely, the final scenes of a traditional tragedy. The sense of suffering, cruelty and waste, the slow death of people and of the created world – the vision outlined earlier in this chapter – amounts to what may be called a 'tragic sense of life'. The tones and gestures, as well as the structure and the ideology, of the play repeatedly parody traditional tragedy. Nevertheless, a 'majestic sadness' (which Racine found essential in tragedy) is a constant burden in the play. Hamm's role as dying king, already mentioned, carries distinct echoes of Shakespearian kings: Lear, Richard II and that kingly magician, Prospero. The allusions to lost power and magnificence, the pains of dispossession and of losing (though loss is finally desired) are all there. The final phase is a long ceremony of self-divestment, as Hamm one-by-one abandons his grotesque symbols of power (or impotence): the gaff, the dog, the whistle, his own face. The player-king moves through abdication to a rehearsal of proper dying. He mimes 'the old style' of a tragic ending.

It is up to each reader or spectator to judge the final effect of *Endgame* – probably a complex of emotions. Yet is it not likely that a certain pity and terror (or awe) will accompany the ending of *Endgame*, despite its lack of a tragic plot? Development and catastrophe give way to something more shadowy: the gestures and tones that allude to tragic action. Consider, for example, the formal ending. From a strictly structural point of view, there is nothing inevitable about the timing – and the placing – of Hamm's imperious announcement 'It's the end, Clov, we've come to the end. I don't need you any more' (p. 50). There is behind this statement no actional pressure to compare with, say, Mark Antony's 'I am dying, Egypt, dying: give me some wine and let me speak a little' (*Antony and Cleopatra*, IV.xiii); after conclusive defeat in battle and self-esteem, inevitable death by suicide. Yet, Hamm's pronouncement has all the resonances of a tragic mode of ending; and all the repeated utterances of the end-motif in the total language of the play build up and point to that final renunciation. It is immediately preceded by the sighting of the 'small boy' by Clov (an episode that is very short in the final English version of the play). And it is succeeded by those conspicuous examples of tragic departure, recognition and self-dispossession – Clov's parting speech and Hamm's final soliloquy. The pathos of that formal ending – only three pages of text – is cumulative and has some of the features of a musical score that can be fully realised and felt only in performance.

Further reflection on *Endgame* as a kind of modern tragedy will also show some of the unique aspects of the play in terms of ideology and structure. It will be noticed that *Endgame* does not offer the final consolation or synthesis of Greek and Shakespearian tragedy. At the end of the *Oresteia* of Aeschylus peace is established between the destructive and the order-seeking forces, in the name of god-given justice in Athens. And at the end of *Macbeth* a measure of political, social and spiritual order is re-established with the purging of the unnatural murders and usurpation of Macbeth. Those endings represent simple conclusions of an otherwise complex tragic pattern, valued by most writers on tragedy from Aristotle to Bradley and beyond. *Endgame* may move us, but never 'console' us; there is no attempt to take the suffering witnessed to the other side of despair. The lack of a final reconciliation contributes to making *Endgame* an 'absurd' play rather than a tragedy in the full sense, and it ties up with the universalising pessimism, the nihilistic strand in the whole of Beckett's work (see pp. 13–15, 157–8).

The cyclic structure, too, goes against all known forms of traditional tragedy; yet it also contributes to a new kind of tragic theatricality. The play-motif ('Me to play'), which opens and closes Hamm's performance of his own slow movement towards death, is, among other things, an enactment of the cycle: 'the end is in the beginning and yet you go on' (p. 44). The 'yet' in this sentence sums up a tragic and non-rational necessity: the need to go on acting, performing. (The ambiguity of 'acting' is deliberately translated into role-playing.) The cycle is running down, as usual in Beckett: it is really a curve that approximates but never reaches base, an asymptotic curve. What is new in *Endgame* is that there is only one cycle, presumably to emphasise the enclosed and final aspect of the cycle (whereas the repeated cycle of *Godot* emphasises the ongoing, potentially infinite series (see chapter 2, p. 28). The one-act structure was reached after much thought and re-writing, as can be seen from Beckett's two-act first and second drafts for *Fin de Partie*, the French text of *Endgame*. The text we know has a greater economy and a more precise focus on the two major strands of 'playing' and 'ending', with the suggestion of a 'day like any other day' (p. 33): a long day with memories of a constantly evoked past and expectations of a far-off/near closing moment. In short, the one-act cyclic structure embodies the sense of an 'everlasting day', long-and-short, static-and-moving.

Another significant feature of the structure of *Endgame* is its use of the short scene as the unit, and of its merging of a succession of scenes, with the breaks omitted, so that the audience would hardly notice the transitions. The scenes build sequences not according to any line of development, but through 'variations on a theme' (playing *and* ending). This can be seen from Beckett's instructions for the Berlin production of *Endgame* in 1967, identifying sixteen scenes as the units of the play's structure:

1 Clov's mime and first monologue.
2 Hamm's awakening, his first monologue, and his first dialogue.
3 The Nagg–Nell dialogue.
4 Hamm–Clov dialogue, with Hamm's first turn around the room.
5 Clov's comic business with the ladder and the telescope.
6 Hamm's questioning of Clov with the burlesque flea scene.
7 Hamm–Clov dialogue with the toy dog scene.
8 Clov's rebellion, Hamm's story of the madman, and the alarm-clock scene.
9 Hamm's story.
10 The prayer ending with Nagg's curse.
11 Hamm's story continued.
12 Hamm's second turn around the room.
13 Hamm–Clov dialogue (farewell).
14 Hamm's role.
15 Clov's closing monologue and exit.
16 Hamm's final monologue.[2]

These notes can be, and have been, given further elaboration but they are probably most useful (to the director as well as to the student) as they stand. If anything, we need a simple pointer to the overall design. Then we can see that the opening and the closing tableaux (scenes 1 and 16 in Beckett's notes) constitute a kind of prologue and epilogue, arranged with approximate symmetry. Scenes 2–10 are dominated by the Hamm–Clov relationship and may be considered to form the first major movement of the play, reaching a climax in the lines borrowed from the *Tempest*: 'Our revels here are nearly ended!' (see above, p. 50). The remaining scenes, 11–15, are dominated by preparing for the end, with the final parting of Clov, in a pattern of repetition and run-down.

Across the formal design, important for Beckett, we glimpse a pattern of tragicomic counterpoint, less broad than in *Godot*, but often unexpected and funny. The black comedy is sharpest at points of tension and lyricism. For instance, Nagg interrupts his mock-nostalgic dialogue with Nell by telling the old Jewish joke about the tailor and the trousers (which took longer to get right than the creation of the world). The bitter questioning of 'meaning' is immediately followed by the farcical flea episode. The story of the madman who thought the end of the world had come, and the ensuing dialogue on Clov's way of leaving, is balanced by the alarm-clock episode – 'the end is terrific'. Clearly, these effects are not just for comic relief, but point to the existential pairing of pain-ridden and laughter-giving experience. The expectation of a grand apocalypse is being parodied by a kind of Lilliputian creation myth with its own doomsday paraphernalia (the flea, the alarm clock). In short, something like the consistently imaginative comic counterpoint of the hell porter in *Macbeth* – who is not just drunk and bawdy but who rehearses some of the tragedy's keywords – is here extended to run through the texture of the whole play.

The comic counterpoint intensifies the theatricality of *Endgame* and is closely allied to explicit references to the theatre – in gestures and phrases that call attention to the act of performance (see also chapter 2, pp. 44–5). Placed at the centre of the scene in which Hamm goes on his first inspection tour around the room (with Clov doing the actual inspecting of the world out there), Clov deliberately lets the telescope fall in clown-play, picks it up again, and turns it on the auditorium:

> I see . . . a multitude . . . in transports . . . of joy.
> (*Pause.*) That's what I call a magnifier. (*He lowers the telescope, turns towards Hamm.*) Well? Don't we laugh?   (p. 25)

The direct reference to the audience is paralleled by attention-raising pointers to the art of play-writing itself, all of them comic parodic. Thus the answer to Clov's at once emotional and reasonable-seeming question 'What is there to keep me here?' is Hamm's 'The dialogue'. And this exchange is followed by one of the best-sustained 'canters' of mock-theatre in which Clov acts as stooge to Hamm's story-telling urge, prompting and urging, questioning and dutifully laughing (discussing what brought on the burst of laughter, pp. 39–40). Beckett has succeeded in theatricalising the condition of the character prone to monologue (that is, the self-reflecting narrator we meet in Beckett's novels). The monologue is transformed into dialogue, the self-conscious tone into 'theatre voices' – voices acting out an act. The same goes for Hamm's elaborate preparations for his final soliloquy (p. 49). Clov interrupts Hamm's sonorous rhetoric of the self ('And me? Did anyone ever have pity on me?') at an early stage; at which Hamm snaps angrily:

> An aside, ape! Did you never hear an aside before?
> (*Pause.*) I'm warming up for my last soliloquy.

In the same vein, Clov's merest suggestion that he has spotted something 'out there', in the void, with his telescope, prompts Hamm's theatre-conscious note of horror: 'More complications! . . . Not an underplot, I trust.'

This degree of internal theatricality keeps the audience at a deliberate distance while it simultaneously parodies the existential and the staged situation. As a distancing device it may be con. trasted with the broad effects of Brecht's theatre, which displays signposts to a scene, reminding the audience that a play is being staged, worked out. Beckett refers to the stage in a unique way: to point to the tragicomic play of isolated minds. This theatricality is further intensified by a subtle network of visual and sound effects which cut into the verbal texture of the play at every point. The role-playing corresponds to gestures and movements, from the long opening mime on. (The stage directions should be carefully read by anyone who has not yet seen the play in performance, to recreate in the imagination at least some of the effects of that long silence.)

We have already noted the recurrent theatrical echoes written into almost every speech in the play, speeches such as 'Can there be misery (*he yawns*) – loftier than mine? No doubt. Formerly. But now? (*Pause.*)' Hamm's speeches can be effectively intoned to sound sonorous or pompous at times (like Pozzo's speeches in *Godot*), while the duets of Nagg and Nell lend themselves to chanting, in a highly stylised senile quaver. We have also noted the sustained rhythmic beat in the play, like the constant pattering of Clov's feet. The combined vision-sound-word texture of *Endgame* calls out for performance in a way that is unique in modern drama. Writers who are primarily concerned with universal situations of inner states or a poetic text (ranging from Sartre among the French existentialists and Maeterlinck, Yeats and Eliot among the one-time masters of inwardness and poetic drama) have not always managed to achieve such a theatrical immediacy. *Endgame* enacts a diminished theatre, along with the diminished human and physical universe it evokes. But it compresses entire worlds of experience out of what Beckett once called 'fundamental sounds' (in a letter concerning *Endgame*, written to Alan Schneider, the play's New York director, dated 29 December 1957): 'My work is a matter of fundamental sounds (no joke intended) made as fully as possible.'

4

Krapp's Last Tape

Krapp's Last Tape (1958) represents two major changes in the formal evolution of Beckett's plays. It is the first embodiment of the isolated person and mind in a new form of monodrama: one character enacting a kind of dialogue between his old and younger selves. And it is the first use of the tape-recorder as the structural pivot of the play. (The tape-recorder was such a recent invention that Beckett had not even seen one at the time the play was written; the opening stage directions provide for a setting in the future, so as to foil the objection that *young* Krapp could not possibly have tape-recorded his birthday memoirs.) We see, then, a further diminishment of drama as traditionally conceived (in terms of character and action) alongside an ingenious new development in dramatic technique, leading to both initial surprise and final effectiveness in the play.

While the formal innovation just mentioned cannot be separated from the emotional power of the play, we need to reflect, first of all, on the human situation that this short play dramatises. The essentially simple existential elements are those found elsewhere in Beckett's work: the deepening isolation of the self, the mind, in the course of a lifetime. Young Krapp still has a whole galaxy of illusions to prop up his vanity: company, glimpses of beautiful women with 'incomparable' eyes or bosom; plans of writing something great – a *magnum opus*; the luxury of judging his still younger self from newly reached moral heights; and the capacity for experiencing a great 'vision', expressed in high-toned lyrical prose and recorded in a sonorous voice with undertones of intellectual pride. Against this, old Krapp has withdrawn into an almost total solitude with sordid habits which include residual whoring, drinking and the excessive consumption of bananas, to boost his shrunken self-esteem. But his delight in words (the word 'spool') remains. The rest is decaying memory contending with the mechanically fixed 'memory' replayed on the tape-recorder: his mother's death, the last tender episode in a story of lost love, and fragments of other recorded experience now without meaning for him.

As this account suggests, *Krapp's Last Tape* is, in many respects, a play of personal diminishment, with a strong yet tender erotic thread not met in Beckett's previous plays, but counter-balanced, here too, by parody and self-mockery. Gone are the cosmic dimensions and the 'clawing', compressed text of *Endgame*, and the 'all the world's a stage' universality of *Waiting for Godot*. We are to contemplate the drama of the isolated self through focusing on an old man's canned memories, interlaced with his ironic comments. It is a miniaturised autobiography, as if seen in a photo-finish, as if performed by himself for himself – unaware of the audience in the theatre.

A dialogue of selves

The play is written for one actor, but there are two voices: Krapp-now (sixty-nine) and Krapp-then (thirty-nine), who criticizes a still younger Krapp's self-recording. The interplay between the living and the canned voices across the passage of time is ingeniously structured, and sets up painfully ironic tensions, repetitions and echoes.

The opening section is no more than a catalogue read out, setting up an immediate series of tragicomic contrasts: between the archaic ledger and the (then) ultra-modern tape-recorder; between the aged, decrepit, clown-like figure and his initial briskness and eagerness, his delight in some of the tapes. Old Krapp's inability to remember what must have been key experiences in his life, 'the black ball' and a 'memorable equinox' (memorable but forgotten all the same), immediately establishes his present decrepitude. His young self is a strange, even obscure identity out there, to be studied as it is summoned, not organically, from memory, but mechanically, from the thirty-year-old tape. 'Farewell to – (*he turns page*) – love' (the pause has a debunking effect) announces the speaker's deliberate search for peak experiences from his youth, remembrance of things past (to use the English title of the novel by Proust which Beckett had studied and written about as early as 1930–1).

The first tape introduces a high-toned 'retrospect': the year that is gone recorded by Krapp on his thirty-ninth birthday. It is self-assured even when self-critical, in keeping with the strong, rather pompous voice called for by the stage direction. Characteristically, he sees himself as being 'at the . . . (*hesitates*) crest of the wave – or thereabouts', and is self-indulgent towards his weaknesses, eating too many bananas and drinking too much (a recurrent comic motif: the youngest Krapp on record spent 'say forty per cent of his waking life' on licensed premises).

But this racy tone modulates into the quiet voice in search of the inner self – characteristic of Krapp as it is of Beckett as writer. It is first heard speaking of significant moments, alone in the darkness of his 'den': 'separating the grain from the husks'. This image is important enough for young Krapp to repeat and interpret:

I suppose I mean those things worth having when all the dust has – when all *my* dust has settled. I close my eyes and try and imagine them.

(p. 12)

We note that this need to find the essential moments in memory is also what now makes old Krapp select particular episodes from the tapes. Even though his present situation is static, as are the events in his recorded memories (fixed for all time in a certain order), Krapp is no passive listener, but his own 'programmer', re-arranging his minimal autobiography. Young Krapp already dwells on darkness and on silence: 'Extraordinary silence this evening. I strain my ears and do not hear a sound' (p. 12). Silence is an important reality in his life; at the same time, the evocation of silence is also a mood-setter in time present, for the perform-ance of the tapes/the last tape.

The inclusion, in the thirty-nine-year-old Krapp's tape, of critical comments on a tape recorded some ten or twelve years earlier, is masterly. For this reveals, for the first time, the irony of a man taking a superior position towards his younger self while his behaviour, as recorded, has not changed in any significant way. He is relieved that a certain love affair is over (Bianca), he ridicules his one-time aspirations and resolutions (here the mechanical and the live laughter of the two Krapps are syn-chronised), and 'he sneers at what he calls his youth and thanks God it's over'. The audience will observe that Krapp at thirty-nine has recorded experiences that are to recur (and to serve as mockery) in later life: the failed love affair and the failed aspira-tions. The habit of sneering at a younger self also persists unto the last tape. The seeming interaction between the three stages of Krapp's life thus suggests a self-repeating series, comparable to the cyclic repetition of the earlier plays. It is like seeing a face endlessly reflected between two mirrors. The rest of the tape is organised around the three significant memories – or 'moments'

– which were cryptically announced by Krapp in the titles read from the ledger: the black ball story commemorating his mother's death; his new vision in the storm on the night of a 'memorable equinox'; and 'farewell to love' presented as a gentle but obsessive love scene. The latter is given prominence by Krapp's impatient editorial control over the tape, through his urgency in choosing, finding and finally re-playing that particular scene.

The story of his mother's death is told with controlled indirection whereby all the emotion is carried by concrete images ('moments') and not by any explicit expression of, for example, the son's feelings towards the mother. Over half the episode is given over to talking about the setting: 'the bench by the weir' from where he could watch his mother's window. The long period of waiting is filled with the fauna of the park world which *fits* the vanished world of Krapp (as it does the world of Beckett): a more or less empty place, suddenly crossed by a nursemaid, 'all white and starch, incomparable bosom', who threatens to call a policeman when Krapp speaks to her. The little scene is not frivolous, for it links up with the thread of 'beautiful women' which cuts through all Krapp's memories, and it also creates a local reality of ordinary living while someone is dying. The moment of death is marked by that once universal image – 'the blind went down'. (That custom to mark a death is now so little observed that members of an audience may miss the point, and so the point of the next, purely private, image of the black ball.) There is no direct grief here, only a patient recording of the stillness slowly moving into action: his holding on 'for a few moments' to that black ball, and finally giving it to the little white dog. It is a perfectly visual – even cinematic – scene evoked by the slow-moving, almost static language. The presentation of such a *stilled narrative* is rare in drama, as rare as the indirect, detached presentation of the experience of a mother's death. (Grief is one of the old emotions that has survived in our culture, even if ritual mourning and the mode of elegy have almost vanished. Audiences may conclude that Krapp's detachment in recording a death is not the norm, but still a felt and dignified occasion.)

From the point of view of Krapp, as presenter of fragments of his life to himself, the sequence on his 'vision' – in early middle age – is to be switched off, impatiently, with a curse followed by a louder curse, until the desired tender scene is reached. The audience may be sufficiently influenced by Krapp's sole mastery over his tape to push the whole reflective sequence into the background. However, the fragments played deserve attention. For in the midst of the purple prose description of the view from the stormy jetty (the style is a mark of young Krapp as minor poet aspiring to greatness) something that sounds like significant self-revelation does try to break through:

What I suddenly saw then was this, that the belief I had been going on all my life, namely – (KRAPP *switches off impatiently, winds tape forward, switches on again*) – great granite rocks the foam flying up into the light of the lighthouse and the wind-gauge spinning like a propeller, clear to me at last that the dark I have always struggled to keep under is in reality my most –

What is it that is suddenly clear to young Krapp? And why is he suppressing it (apart from the urgent wish to get on to the erotic episode)? The unfinished sentence is so constructed as to make some kind of conclusion possible: 'is in reality my most' . . . valuable source of inspiration. Some such phrase would balance the sentence grammatically and semantically. But now Krapp has lost interest in the vision that once seemed a turning point in his creative life. It is like forgetting a discovery, a word (the word 'viduity' or the associations of 'memorable equinox'). For Krapp to lose the significance of a major spiritual insight (in a year otherwise marked by 'profound gloom and indigence'), reaches the tragic pole in his otherwise tragicomic diminishment – comparable to his failure in art, and his failure in love, explicitly recorded in both the tapes played. And beyond the point of view and condition of Krapp, the insight concerning the dark ('that the dark I have always struggled to keep under is in reality my most – ') links up with the keynote of darkness, and the associated imagery of loss and isolation, which runs throughout Beckett's whole work. It is as if the author had transferred one of his key experiences to Krapp, in a play that almost certainly has an unusual autobiographical dimension (see Introduction).

The episode in the punt is also unusual, both in subject and tone, in Beckett's drama. Though it is a 'farewell scene' in a failed relationship, it is a tender love idyll, presented in simple and direct lyricism, without irony or interruption from Krapp, young or old. (The later, coarse counterblast from old Krapp is ambivalent.) Not only is the scene centrally placed by Krapp as the one memory worth seeking out and re-playing – in search of self-restoration, perhaps – but it is also among the most memorable scenes in Beckett's theatre. The scene is almost com-

71

pletely static, a reflective stilling of the world in and through a
moment.

We drifted in among the flags and stuck. The way they went down,
sighing, before the stem! (*Pause.*) I lay down across her with my face in
her breasts and my hand on her. We lay there without moving. But under
us all moved, and moved us, gently, up and down, and from side to
side.

This is a 'still point', a moment held for a lifetime, rather than a
'crisis' in loving. What is more, it is told from Krapp's point of
view, almost entirely shutting out the *nameless* girl as an independent female personality. Almost. For there is one point where the
voice of that girl can be heard (the only direct speech, the only
'non-Krapp' speech in the whole play): 'I noticed a scratch on her
thigh and asked her how she came by it. Picking gooseberries, she
said.' In that light, cheeky, repartee a moment of erotic dialogue
emerges in Krapp's otherwise self-imprisoned monologue: the
portrait and the idiom of a young woman Krapp must have loved
once, however transiently. The episode recorded is the only one
on the tape that speaks of a true encounter, and not just glimpses
of beautiful object-like women. (The evocation of eyes.)
　　Listening to that record, old Krapp's first impulse is to reject
the feeling if not the memory: through denigrating his former self.
It amounts to a virtual dialogue between the two selves, the living
voice 'answering' the fixed, mechanical, younger voice. And that
dialogue is internalised in the two voices of the old man's consciousness, one rejecting, the other affirming, a possibly authentic
moment of love:

A: Just been listening to that stupid bastard I took myself for thirty years
　　ago, hard to believe I ever was as bad as that. Thank God
　　that's all done with anyway. (*Pause.*)
B: The eyes she had! [. . .] Everything there, everything on this old
　　muckball, all the light and dark and famine and feasting of
　　. . . (*hesitates*) the ages! (*In a shout.*) Yes!
A: Let that go. Jesus! Take his mind off his homework! Jesus! (*Pause.*
　　Weary.)
B: Ah well, maybe he was right. (*Pause.*) Maybe he was right. (*Broods.*)
　　　　　　　　　　　　　　　　　　　　　　　　　　　(pp. 16–17)

The rest of old Krapp's soliloquy (which is to be his *last* tape)
speaks, without pathos, of the repetition and diminishment
brought by ageing: spiritual exhaustion ('nothing to say not a

squeak'), indigestion and constipation; his lack of success as an author ('seventeen copies sold'); his death-wish; his romantic love fantasy through fiction (crying over Effie, the heroine of the German novel *Effie Briest* [*sic*]) along with an old man's semi-impotent lechery ('Fanny came in . . .'). The rueful meditation on the failures of self lead to his singing of the hymn 'Now the day is over', and to the final self-apostrophe: 'Be again!'

That four-times-repeated phrase, 'Be again', has the double irony of Krapp's divided feelings and his self-mocking situation. The feeling is intensely ambivalent: rejection through the deliberate banality in naming the props of happiness ('Be again in the dingle on a Christmas eve . . .') or simply denigrating his life, 'All that misery'; at the same time the rhetorical tone expresses, beyond what we call nostalgia, a painful sense of waste, as in the final recognition scene of a tragedy. The self-apostrophising mode is in itself, clearly, 'a waste of time', as the replay of his favourite tape is a 'pathetic' substitute for being. (At this point Krapp can be seen as resembling the average man looking at the family photographs, as well as the potential poet contemplating a failed work from which a fragment has been carved out for solo performance.)

The repetition of young Krapp's tape at the end of the play, separated from the *last* tape by a long pause and impatient re-selection, is again masterly. The moment shared with a girl in the punt – the one person who emerges from Krapp's taped solo as an authentic voice, *not his*, even though quoted and taped by him – sharpens the isolation of the listening old man. The audience – almost certainly moved on the emotional/lyrical level – has its response to the tape reinforced. At the same time, the additional material, the ten short concluding sentences played slowly, quietly, between two pauses, and fading into the long final silence, provides a sad, ironic frame. The past and the present fuse in old Krapp as listener to young Krapp as performer. The old man's silence is that of total isolation merging, for a moment, with the total silence evoked in the tape. Then the young man's confident 'peak experience' and self-appraisal – the concluding words of the taped text, as of the play – sound vain, in the strong biblical sense of 'vanity . . . all is vanity':

Perhaps my best years are gone. When there was a chance of happiness. But I wouldn't want them back. Not with the fire in me now. No, I wouldn't want them back.

The audience hears 'the fire in me now', its grand resonances contrasting with the decrepit old man motionlessly staring before him. The final irony is completed in word, image, gesture and silence – an achieved synchronisation of theatre effects.

Theatre

A relatively short monodrama which is the vehicle of memory (rather than internal conflict or the re-enactment of past action) is not the kind of play we would expect to require, and to work well in, stage performance. Yet, as the foregoing discussion has tried to show, this text too is complete only when the various kinds of auditive and visual counterpoints are fully perceived. The subtle yet strong counterpoint of the end is the most memorable instance of the extent to which Beckett has succeeded in theatricalising a voice, a retrospective, reflective, soliloquising voice. For a start, the presence of the actor as 'decrepit old man' is in itself a counterpoint: the face, the unstable, shuffling walk, as much as the rasping voice with the grunts and occasional groans. The reader can imagine it, but can hardly create the impact (excelled only by the impact of Winnie's buried body in the later *Happy Days*).

The opening silence is as significant as the closing one. It is that long silent action (a miniature mime-play controlled by one of Beckett's longest stage directions) which creates the sensation of Krapp's isolation as well as his 'bodily decrepitude'. A series of semi-senile games are performed: the game of searching for the key, the game of opening and locking drawers, the banana-eating game, the inevitable near-fall (the clown), the popping of cork and the carrying of a ledger to the table. All this is minimal action and yet it is, we realise, the full round of Krapp's day, of his present life. In other words, the opening of the play recreates for the audience that degree of extreme isolation which traditional drama reserved for its final scene – for example, King Richard II alone in his prison cell, his soliloquy turning into a dialogue of selves.

Krapp is not only a stylised old man; the role is further stylised to give him an aspect of the clown: white face, purple nose. (Other roles in Beckett's drama have clown aspects, notably Clov in *Endgame*: the fusion of naturalistic and stylised elements in the role has the effect of fusing a music-hall monologue with a mime-play.) The role then creates pathos and satire, sympathy and laughter, throughout the performance – in keeping with Beckett's double style, shifting from the lyrical to the broadly rhetorical (as in the scene discussed above).

The placing of Krapp in his 'den' is also significantly pointed by the lighting: he occupies a small lighted area beyond which objects recede into the darkness. The back room may be just visible, giving Krapp a goal to reach – the treasure-house of bottles – while his shuffling towards and from that goal provides a counter-point to his otherwise rigidly sedentary posture.

Krapp's total involvement with the tape-recorder – his substitute memory – is strikingly enacted in the noise and business of managing it (over and above playing the tape itself). We are back in the early technology of the tape-recorder with its reels, far less easy to manipulate than the later cassette-recorders. And Krapp, though not exaggeratedly clumsy, is sufficiently impatient and semi-skilled to show off the disadvantages of his machine: the time taken with finding the reel and placing it in position, the winding forward and back with attendant whining and whirring sounds; the athletic struggle with the sheer accumulation of material: spools, snake-like tapes, the microphone, the switches.

Facial expressions are also exceptionally significant in this play, registering sudden shifts of mood, ranging from ecstasy (over the word 'spool') to the subdued yet visible signs of habitual suffering brought on by long isolation. This aspect of the performance is probably even more effective in television – in close-up – than in the theatre, as anyone who has seen Patrick Magee in the role of Krapp (Channel 4, December 1982) can testify: this actor had something like 'confirmed desperation' written into his features, but expressed a variety of other emotions – including serenity in the river episode – over that base. During substantial periods of play-time that face was sweating, thereby enhancing a physicality that was almost repellent, though also capable of evoking compassion (the beads of sweat resembled tears). But while individual actors can and do give an added dimension to *Krapp's Last Tape*, this is only possible because in this play, as elsewhere, Beckett has thought through his verbal text – with all its nuances – in terms of image and sound and movement, in short in overall and interacting design.

5

Happy Days

At first sight, *Happy Days* appears to have several features which significantly change, if not reverse and parody, the remorseless worlds of the preceding plays. Winnie, who dominates the play, is an average, world-loving woman as against the decaying male intellectuals who keep recurring in the earlier plays (Nell in *Endgame* is the only previous female character). Winnie's optimistic chatter can also be contrasted with the frequently life-denying, nihilistic utterances of protagonists in the other plays. Winnie's tone of voice often rises from cheerful to exuberant, from little phrases of consolation to fragments of prayer, hymns of praise, lyric poetry and a song: her performance makes us almost forget that the speaker is buried in a mound of earth. Blazing light illuminates the stage in contrast to the dark interiors of *Endgame* and *Krapp's Last Tape*; and the stage may be seen to be open to infinite space while the two earlier plays mentioned have closed prison-cell-like scenery. It takes time for the reader or the audience to realise that the blazing light may be a form of 'hellish light' and that the open expanses of space may point only to infinite empti-ness. It also takes time to become fully aware of the terrible irony in Winnie's praise for the created world.

That terrible irony – an enchanted voice tied to a dying body – links up with other family resemblances to the preceding plays. Winnie's immobility recalls Hamm's wheelchair, now taken to an extreme, dream-like or symbolic point. Her constant, spontaneous-seeming chatter may appear to be the live counter-part of Krapp's canned memories, interior monologues played back to gain some kind of control over time and the decay of personality. The running down of Winnie's over-heated universe has its parallel in the dying universe seen from the cell windows of *Endgame*. Winnie's struggle to pass the time – by cherishing objects and phrases, an old toothbrush and fine quotations – can be seen as variations of the 'waiting' and 'ending' games in Beckett's two full-length plays. Her unending flow of speech – pitted against a physical and mental void – also recalls the earlier plays. Finally, the two-act structure, with its repetitions and symmetries, can suggest an infinite series or the narrowing turns of a wheel, a variation on the *Waiting for Godot* structure.

The celebration of decay and survival

The opening section of *Happy Days* (about three pages of text, a few minutes of performance time) presents an epitome of the play: the persistent fears and consolations of Winnie. She begins with words of praise: 'Another heavenly day' and fragments of a prayer invoking Jesus Christ and the eternal world. Her first personal utterance is a call to her unseen partner, introduced as 'poor Willie'. There follow, in rapid succession, the threads of three discomforts: the tube of toothpaste is running out; her teeth are in bad condition; and Willie, her partner for life, has no zest left for anything. These three threads of distress are subtly interwoven with three threads of corresponding consolation: 'can't be helped' or 'just can't be cured'; 'no change . . . no pain'; and Willie's 'marvellous gift' of being able to go on sleeping 'for ever'. Consolations are in turn accompanied by feelings of inadequacy and fear (Winnie's failure to read the writing on the toothbrush brings panic at the thought that she may be going blind) leading to further consolation, through her quotation of a fragment from the classics on the sorrows of seeing: 'Woe, woe is me – to see what I see' and the invocation of the blind Milton's 'holy light'. But her awareness of light, excess light, brings a new terror: 'blaze of hellish light'. That fear is countered, for a moment, by a further series of commonplace phrases for cheering herself up: 'can't complain' . . . 'mustn't complain' . . . 'so much to be thankful for . . . no pain'.

These sudden fluctuations define Winnie's titanic struggle in her paradoxical ecstasy of suffering. The main theme is introduced at the beginning and, as in a sonata, subtle variations on that theme are worked out throughout the two acts of the play.

Winnie is exposed to extreme deprivation from the start, yet her condition deteriorates: by Act II she is buried up to her neck and she appears to be losing her companion. Nevertheless, her endless monologue affirms continuity and an acceptable existence: 'no change . . . no pain'. It is as if a figure from Dante's *Inferno* had to endure endless torture while praising a private vision of paradise. The audience sees something of the torture and nothing of paradise – but hears the words of praise. The causes of torment, and its duration, are never revealed. In this way the play creates a mythic dimension for the humble woman trying to get through her minimal day with as much grace as possible. Thus the mundane and the mythic are counterpointed, and both levels are then worked out in cycles of recurrent images: the handicapped woman coping with left-over possessions, words and memories, in a desert of solitude accompanied by a barely present companion; and Everywoman as the victim of a universe without any sign of Providence, full of speculations about that universe and her own perplexing destiny.

To see this pattern clearly we must look at the main threads in Winnie's unending monologue. First, the consolation of objects. From the opening on we see Winnie's fascination with the toothbrush, and the undecipherable writing on it. As Act I progresses that object gets more and more attention, and the process of deciphering the writing is experienced by Winnie as a discovery. Like the archaeologist who has finally established the 'message' in runic or cuneiform script, Winnie's words turn the commonplace toothbrush into an instrument of (parodic) illumination: 'fully guaranteed . . . genuine pure . . . hog's setae' (that is, hog's bristle, the rare word was substituted for the common one in the final version of the play). Both the process and the result of discovery seem delightful to her: the writing on the toothbrush is like the 'old style' which points to a vanished world now recalled for comfort. The instructions on the medicine bottle served a similar purpose. And these chance writings – like 'found poems' – in turn link up with Winnie's relish of quotations from the classics. But wordless objects hold her attention too – all the contents of her capacious bag, and the parasol – like trophies left over from a previous existence, on a once-normal earth. The mirror and the lipstick with the poetic names, 'Ensign crimson' and 'Pale flag', poignantly remind Winnie and the audience of her faded physical beauty and of the persistence of vanity in this desert. (The opening stage directions stress her physical appearance: 'about fifty, well-preserved, blonde for preference, plump, arms and shoulders bare, low bodice, big bosom, pearl necklace'. The ageing popular star, a little vulgar but holding on to dignity, is partly suggested by these visual signs (see pp. 83–5).)

She is trying to please, but whom? Willie? An unknown audience out there? Herself? A vanished ideal of fashion, in keeping with the 'old style'? Certainly her daily ritual is a way of keeping up appearances, but also a way of ordering the otherwise infinite wastes of time. Her attention (and Beckett's emphatic stage time) is given to her fineries, item by item. Her hat is no simple protection against the heat of the day; it is ornate with a crumpled feather, incongruous in its worn elegance. Her spectacles provide another occasion for looking at herself in the mirror each time they are adjusted, in a comforting little routine: taken off, polished, put on once more. Like the contemplation of the toothbrush it helps to structure Winnie's empty hours. Her revolver is a more sinister object, explicitly pointing to possible suicide ('Take it away, Winnie, take it away, before I put myself out of my misery', Willie used to say to her, p. 26). However, we sense that Winnie's extreme situation cannot be resolved by suicide, and the revolver has become just another domesticated object, affectionately addressed as 'Brownie' – punning on the name and optimism of the poet Browning. Finally, the parasol also suggests bygone elegance, a prop that turns into a threat when it is suddenly burned up by the hellish heat of the place. Its unfurling is another ritual (p. 27) and its magical restoration of Winnie at the beginning of Act II draws attention to the surrealistic, so to speak extra-terrestrial, location of the play.

Beyond the accumulation of left-over objects is the surrounding physical and cosmic world that holds Winnie as prisoner. The spectator (though not every reader) is constantly aware of Winnie's reduced and immobilised state. But the physical features, of Hell – the heat, the paralysis of life, the implacable pull of the earth – are not immediately present in terms of scenic effect. Our theatre art cannot easily simulate heat, especially as Winnie, according to her own reporting, no longer feels the rising heat and perspires less (pp. 27–8). So we get our 'readings' of this harsh universe from Winnie's running commentary, woven into the other topics that give her long day a pattern. Such is the burning heat that it is a consolation for Winnie to look forward to: 'the happy day to come when flesh melts at so many degrees' (p. 16); and the burning up of the parasol, mentioned before, is taken for granted as an ordinary phenomenon in *this* world: 'with the sun blazing so much fiercer, is it not natural things should go on fire . . . spontaneous like' (p. 29). The crescendo of heat appears to give way to 'everlasting perishing cold' in Act II (p. 39) – without explanation, 'just chance' thinks Winnie. We may conclude that this universe is either mythic (where extreme heat may well give way to extreme cold, as in the Scandinavian creation myth), or else it is an accelerated version of the cooling down of the universe forecast by our physicists. In any case, Winnie's passing com-

ments on her cosmic environment give her the stature of a mythic
figure – a kind of female Titan struggling against the punishing
gods. Nor is the earth that encompasses her neutral. It presses
against her and tortures her: 'the earth is very tight today, can it
be I have put on flesh, I·trust not' (p. 23). But even this constant
physical discomfort or pain is turned by Winnie into a source of
possible solace, in a curious piece of geological speculation:
'perhaps some day the earth will yield and let me go, the pull is
so great, yes, crack all round me and let me out' (p. 26). In this
earth, as in the world of *Endgame*, nothing grows; yet a comic –
even cosmic – disturbance may be caused by the sudden appearance of a creature, an emmet progressing through the grass.
(In *Endgame* it was a sole surviving flea.) In sum, Winnie's ironic
triumph over her circumstances involves what sounds like a stoical
acceptance of a cruel cosmos.

Winnie cannot exercise the slightest control over the cosmic
change – the decay – all around her. She knows and admits that
her own body is decaying daily, and the ritual celebration of each
new day (the cycle of two days, suggesting infinite time) is a way
of taming the threat of infinity. The stream of commonplace, self-
consoling phrases already mentioned is an essential aspect of her
'survival kit', as everyday clichés may be used like shibboleths or
charms. The oft-repeated little phrases ('that is what I find so
wonderful', 'great mercies', 'so much to be thankful for' and
'no change') are the kind that might well be recommended by
advocates of 'positive thinking', auto-suggestion and faith heal-
ing. To the audience/reader this language of incongruous affirmation no doubt has a constant undertone of irony.

Her phrases are props like her objects and like talking to Willie.
The text provides an ingenious mixing of all these elements, as in
a cloth made up of cross-woven patterns. First let us look at Winnie's 'classics' – the repeated quotations which point to and
express her condition. They are the clearest examples of the 'old
style' offering consolation: the seeming persistence of memory,
identity and words despite bodily decrepitude. The act of recalling
these lines, in fragments, from a weakening memory, is itself a
source of reassurance to Winnie, offering the solace of continuity
('no change') against the fragility of her mind, and the precarious
nature of words.

The abundance of quotations may lead some readers to conclude that we are dealing with a hyper-literary and allusive text,
like Eliot's *Waste Land* ("These fragments I have shored against my

ruins'). But the quotations are not used as pointers to other texts – as literary allusions – but as dramatic symptoms of Winnie's condition. The most memorable quotations speak of 'woe' and 'light'. Moreover, in their fragmented state, interwoven with clichés and cheap language, and ushered in by Winnie's naturalistic, mind-searching phrases ('What are those wonderful lines . . .?'), the 'classics' become an integral part of the text – part of its careful 'old style' lyricism. Winnie's habit of quoting may date the text (and Winnie's world), for quoting from the classics appears to be very much less usual in contemporary culture than it was even one generation ago. So the old-world habit of quoting for consolation and self-expression may be added to the faded paraphernalia of Winnie's objects, to Willie's final costumed bow, in top hat and morning coat, and to *The Merry Widow* tune, as the debris of the 'early-twentieth-century' aspect of a play which, in other respects, aims at metaphors for all time.

Winnie's opening prayer creates a kind of 'holy ground', in the sense of a ritual that can be felt, whether or not the words spring from faith or only from habit. The low-voiced litany – 'World without end Amen' – emerges from the prolonged silence of the opening to usher in the traditional world, 'the old style'. It is immediately punctured by Winnie's twice-repeated loud shout of 'Hoo-oo'. So the vulgar business of coping with the new day's trivial tasks begins in a context suggesting infinite time.

The quoted fragments from the classics similarly evoke at least a time stretching back beyond time present, and they too are words used as a kind of litany against the stream of ordinary babble. The quotations enrich as well as counterpoint Winnie's ordinary language. In any case, they have become part of *her* language, as can be seen from the dramatic use of quotations in which 'woe' (almost archaically literary) is the keyword. The lines console even as they name and express a state of mind, 'a rapture of distress', to borrow a phrase from Auden.

What are those wonderful lines – (*wipes one eye*) – woe is me – (*wipes the other*) – to see what I see – (*looks for spectacles*) – ah yes – (*takes up spectacles*) – wouldn't miss it – (*starts polishing spectacles, breathing on lenses*) – or would I? (*polishes*) holy light – (*polishes*) bob up out of the dark – (*polishes*) blaze of hellish light.   (p. 11)

(*Takes up mirror, starts doing lips.*) What is that wonderful line? (*Lips.*) Oh fleeting joys – (*lips*) – oh something lasting woe. (*Lips. She is interrupted by disturbance from* WILLIE.)   (p. 13)

Oh well, what does it matter, that is what I always say, so long as one
. . . you know . . . what is that wonderful line . . . laughing wild . . .
something something wild amid severest woe. (*Pause.*) And now? (*Long
pause.*)   (pp. 24–5)

It should be clear from the texture of these passages that the
quotations are woven into the flow of Winnie's talk so deftly that
they are both perceived *as* quotations and absorbed as words
among other kindred words. The dynamics of talk, with the
pauses, and the tragicomically appropriate action (wiping one eye,
making up the lips) transform the literary fragments into theatrical
events (see also pp. 83–91). And it hardly matters whether the
audience, or even the reader, recognises the source of these 'woe'
lines (respectively from *Hamlet* III.i: 'O Woe is me, / To have seen
what I have seen, see what I see!'; *Paradise Lost*, Book X, ll.741–2:
O fleeting joys / Of paradise dear bought with lasting woe';
Thomas Gray, *On a Distant Prospect of Eton College*: 'and moody
madness laughing wild / Amid severest woe . . .'). What matters
is the thematic fitness of the lines as they are dredged up from
Winnie's faltering memory. The tragic tone – together with the
inseparable parody of that tone – is likely to make an immediate
impact on any audience. Winnie's classics 'help one through the
day' (p. 43), celebrating her resistance to decay until a time 'when
words must fail' (p. 25).

In addition to reflecting on objects and classical quotations,
Winnie finds time – in her infinite-seeming day – to meditate
on her own identity and ask questions on the nature of self. This
kind of speculation, which is one of the main subjects of Beckett's
novels, clearly carries some risk of excessive soliloquising, for in-
trospection and self-mirroring might submerge the more dynamic
elements of Winnie's speech. How Beckett manages to make even
the most lyrical material dramatic will be discussed in the following section. At the same time, Winnie's reflections are material for
further reflection: the reader/audience is challenged (as in the
Elizabethan soliloquy) to think about one of the most painful
paradoxes of living: the conscious sense of identity even as the
whole body–mind can be seen and felt to decay.

Then . . . now . . . what difficulties here, for the mind. (*Pause.*) To have
always been what I am – and so changed from what I was. (*Pause.*)

This is not an abstract speculation: it springs from Winnie's
situation. and is inexorably embodied in her. The philosophising

woman is still the 'ordinary woman' given to much talk and thinking about the contradictions of living – while dying. Her world
of thoughts and talk is a source of inexhaustible consolation for
Winnie, even though consciousness (for a person suffering in
isolation) might be the source of torment, and talk (for someone
aware of the possibility that there is nobody 'out there' to listen)
might intensify the threat of existential emptiness.

The consolation springs from endowing words – the act of
speaking – with an almost sacred sense; it is a gift: 'Fortunately
I am in tongue again' (p. 28). 'Being in tongue', that non-
colloquial phrase which we might associate with 'speaking in
tongues' (the pentecostal gift of sudden speech which only the initiated can understand), rescues Winnie not only from boredom
but also from isolation. For it is the vehicle for conjuring up company – turning speech-in-the-void into intended conversation.
The person being addressed is, principally, that far from substantial partner, Willie. How this transforms Winnie's monologue into a kind of dialogue we shall see in the next section. Meanwhile
we may note how Winnie's reaching out for company, for an
interlocutor, does not mock her act of speech even though it is
mostly unreciprocated if not illusory:

Not that I flatter myself you hear much, no Willie, God forbid. (*Pause.*)
Days perhaps when you hear nothing. (*Pause.*) But days too when you
answer. (*Pause.*) So that I may say at all times, even when you do not
answer and perhaps hear nothing, something of this is being heard, I am
not merely talking to myself, that is in the wilderness, a thing I could
never bear to do – for any length of time. (*Pause.*) That is what enables
me to go on, go on talking that is. (p. 18)

Theatre and structure

The image of the half-buried woman in the mound of soil can be
placed among the supreme visual metaphors of the modern
theatre. *Happy Days* is probably more dependent on performance,
on immediate visual impact in the theatre, than any other Beckett
play. Seeing Winnie is to experience the savage juxtaposition of
decaying body and affirmative words, from the start to the end of
the play. The rhythmic power of the text, the counterpoint of
words and silences, the variety of speech styles within the long
monologue, can also be tested in a sound recording, while reading
and re-reading is still the only way to study the subtle inter-

weaving of themes. But mere reading requires an unusual degree of imaginative attention to recreate, on the stage of the mind, the introductory stage directions – as well as the visual and auditory 'scoring' throughout the text.

We have here the paradox of an eminently literary/verbal/ abstract writer immersing himself in the concrete elements of theatricality, so that almost every speech in the text has the theatre as its context. There is probably no other stage image in all drama that so dominates the play as Winnie's physical condition *as* immobile and incessant speaker. Even the blindness of Oedipus and the madness of King Lear in the storm are, in terms of action, episodes in the play, however climactic and unforgettable. Winnie in her bondage is omnipresent. The text does not offer any explanation, any 'case history' for this woman's extreme situation. We may contrast this with a short play by Pinter, *A Kind of Alaska* (1984), where a woman wakes from a twenty-year coma or sleeping sickness. Her confused situation and arrested consciousness are subtly dramatised in her speech, but are, nevertheless, explained to the patient, and so to the audience, by the doctor who attends her. In another powerful modern play, Peter Handke's *Kaspar* (1967), the condition of the central character (the boy brought up in total isolation without ever having been taught to speak) is based on a story that has become legendary and which is directly dramatised in the 'crippled' ungrammatical speech of Kaspar. But the story or situation of Winnie is wholly Beckett's invention. As a speaker Winnie is far from handicapped; indeed, some of her speeches are incantatory arias which have inspired such classically trained actresses as Peggy Ashcroft and Madeleine Renaud. So her physical condition (being buried in a desert-like place, in the blaze of a perpetual noon) is expressed, first and foremost, in the visual sign language of the theatre.

The physical diminishment of Winnie between the two acts is the main experience of those who *see* the play: by Act II she has sunk, or has been sucked into, the earth which has an infernal or mythic dimension. (A similar image was used in *Le Chien andalou*, the surrealist film made by Bunuel and Dali in 1929. And a similar brutal deterioration in the interval between the first and the second act is the lot of Pozzo and Lucky.)

When this image is *not* seen, or held constantly before the mind's eye, the patterns of diminishment evoked by words alone tend to get dimmed. For example, Winnie's meditation on the change in her condition – against her repeated claim of 'no change' – gains much of its force from the context, the speaker's situation:

I say I used to pray. (*Pause.*) Yes. I must confess I did. (*Smile.*) Not now. (*Smile broader.*) No no. (*Smile off. Pause.*) Then . . . now . . . what difficulties here, for the mind. To have been always what I am – and so changed from what I was. (*Pause.*) I am the one, I say the one, then the other. (*Pause.*) Now the one, then the other. (*Pause.*)   (p. 38)

Such lyrical speculations about the nature of the self (the oppositions of then/now, I am/I was, the one/the other) gain a terrible clarity from the immediate impact of Winnie's body. Soliloquising, which is in danger of turning into a stream of consciousness, is transformed by Beckett into Winnie's cruel exhibition of her skrinking body:

My arms. (*Pause.*) My breasts. (*Pause.*) What arms? (*Pause.*) What breasts? (*Pause.*)   (p. 38)

Other speculative remarks of Winnie – metaphysical and cosmological – mark the passage of time between the two acts. There is the passing suggestion that universal heat 'might be the eternal cold . . . Everlasting perishing cold' (p. 39) – which sounds like another version of Hell. There is the paradox of supposing Willie dead yet asserting his continued existence – 'you are there' (p. 38) – whether through memory or willed imagination or theatrical illusion. And there is the strange, dream-like image (as if moving beyond purgatory, an intimation of paradise, in Dante's language): 'Eyes float up that seem to close in peace . . . to see . . . in peace' (p. 38). These and other images hint at some kind of change, at the refinement or transmutation of the suffering woman's body–mind. But the hints remain mere hints, are not tied to a structure of change. We may feel that Act II would dissolve in lyricism, and neither the phrases repeated from Act I nor the new phrases would stand out so clearly, if it were not for the theatrical underpinning. We see and hear what does *not* change (the speaker's urge to talk, the loud clamour of the bell and the intense light) against what has changed (the speaker's bodily condition and words). Act II lacks the power of the second act of *Waiting for Godot* in suggesting infinity against the limits of time, repetition and painful change, but it does enact the awesome paradox of changing stillstand, living death.

The absence from Act II of Willie, the life-long partner and the recipient of so many of Winnie's remarks and attentions (see below), reinforces the gradual change – the pathos of dying. But pathos is parodied, pushed towards the grotesque, in the painful clumsiness of Willie's 'final appearance': like a once-competent actor attempting a performance that can only exhibit his present impotence. Again the stage directions need to be imaginatively reconstructed by anyone who has not seen the play: 'He is on all fours, dressed to kill – top hat, morning coat, striped trousers, etc., white gloves in hand. Very long bushy white Battle of Britain moustache. He halts, gazes front, smooths moustache. . . He advances on all fours towards centre, halts, takes off hat and looks up at Winnie. He is now not far from the centre and within her field of vision. Unable to sustain effort of looking up he sinks head to ground' (p. 45).

The deliberately theatrical get-up, the costumed masquerade enacting Willie's last wish to appear as a dashing matinee idol or as ladykiller (as if the senile figure at the end of the 'Seven Ages' speech in *As You Like It* moved back in time to play the role of the young lover) once more underscores the pathos of decrepitude. The whole scene is ironically counterpointed by the singing of Winnie's song (the music-box tune): the once popular and elegant yet now hackneyed and faded hit song from Lehár's *The Merry Widow*, in a climax that is a 'dying fall'. The song itself is simply sentimental, but the total scene is moving as a complex fusion of theatre effects. Willie's last gesture is ambiguous: is he reaching for the revolver or for Winnie? Is he resting or dying? The latter seems more probable in context, but the open-endedness of the ending (the theatrical *tableau*) adds to its impact in performance.

Seen or unseen, Winnie's grotesquely inadequate partner provides the play with most of its direct action or quasi-action, its black comedy, as well as its actual and make-believe dialogue. For Winnie and Willie act out the semblance of a couple and are, like the couples in Beckett's earlier plays, inseparable. Yet they are virtually separated and physically totally out of each other's reach. Physically communicating only through fragments, monosyllables and certain noises: Winnie's initial 'Hoo-oo' and Willie's frequent grunts and groans with occasional guffaws. Such a minimal relationship nevertheless is full of gestures that mime and parody a continuing bond, presumably marriage.

In portraying this incongruous example of marital fidelity, Beckett is again exploiting a theatrical potentiality, mostly that of farce. Winnie and Willie repeatedly suggest certain comic types – despite their extreme situation: the ever-contented, sweetly cooing wife partnered by the grumpy, incommunicative, impotent husband. Audiences tend to laugh at the couple's exchanges, including some of the more grotesque ones – like Willie interrupting one of Winnie's meditations by holding up a postcard – a peculiarly filthy pornographic card, judging from Winnie's shocked outbursts. But her shock is pretended; in her handicapped state she still examines the card, long and carefully, through her glass. Winnie's next attempt at a reflective soliloquy is again interrupted by the reappearance of Willie's hand ('*takes off hat, disappears with hat*', and so on) in a sustained music-hall routine reminiscent of *Waiting for Godot*. As elsewhere in Beckett's drama, the popular stage effect serves to break a lyrical or tender moment; for example, Winnie's memory of Willie praising her 'golden' hair is soon followed by her having to watch Willie's clumsy attempt at crawling back to his hole. One of the sketch-like episodes – the hearing test – is itself a miniature tragicomedy: Winnie's compassionate pleas answered by the crescendo of Willie's irritation and anger. The same short scene also exemplifies Beckett's ability to use one of Winnie's quotations from the classics: 'Fear no more the heat of the sun', from *Cymbeline* IV.ii, in a fully theatrical way.

WINNIE: (*Now in her normal voice, still turned towards him.*) Can you hear me? (*Pause.*) I beseech you, Willie, just yes or no, can you her me, just yes or nothing.
    Pause.
WILLIE: Yes.
WINNIE: (*turning front, same voice*). And now?
WILLIE: (*irritated*). Yes.
WINNIE: (*less loud*). And now?
WILLIE: (*more irritated*). Yes.
WINNIE: (*still less loud*). And now? (*A little louder.*) And now?
WILLIE: (*violently*). Yes!
WINNIE: (*same voice*). Fear no more the heat o' the sun.
    (*Pause.*) Did you hear that?
WILLIE: (*irritated*). Yes.
WINNIE: (*same voice*). What? (*Pause.*) What?
WILLIE: (*more irritated*). Fear no more.
    Pause.
WINNIE: (*same voice*). No more what? (*Pause.*) Fear no more what?
WILLIE: (*violently*) Fear no more!
WINNIE: (*normal voice, gabbled*). Bless you Willie I do appreciate your goodness I know what an effort it costs you, now you may relax I shall not trouble you again unless I am obliged to, by that I mean unless I come to the end of my own resources which is most unlikely, just to know that in theory you can hear me even though in fact you don't is all I need.(pp. 21–2)

This sequence has about it something of a routine marital exchange, with the mixture of caring and exhausted patience given pathos by the obvious fact that Willie's hearing is defective and yet must be celebrated as a good deal 'better than nothing' by Winnie. Her dependence on the remnants of dialogue with her life-long partner is stated by her with explicit irony, repeatedly. This eking out of a relationship – a dialogue – out of minimal fragments of conversation with a minimally present partner, becomes one of the major verbal inventions of the play, distinct from the dialogue of pseudocouples in *Waiting for Godot* and *Endgame* on the one hand, and from the isolated soliloquisers in *Krapp's Last Tape* and *Not I* on the other. Nowhere else has Beckett so sympathetically shown – and parodied – the human need to address another person, a 'YOU', who is no longer capable of proper answers, only of inadequate and haphazard gestures. Thus *Happy Days* is transformed by drawing into itself a stunted but theatrically effective dialogue. The minimal exchanges between Willie and Winnie (not counting the former's reading out loud such grotesquely relevant/irrelevant advertisements as 'Opening for smart youth', p. 14) include: Willie's monosyllabic and funny 'It' in answer to Winnie wondering whether *hair* goes with the plural 'them' or the singular 'it'; his crude punning on emmet's eggs as 'formication', an old man's contrived sex-joke paralleled by his relish of merely saying the word 'sucked up' and by defining the word hog, with pedantic precision (which might well refer to his own state) as 'castrated male swine'. Anyone who has attended a performance of this play will have noticed that such 'one-liners' invariably evoke laughter – they are part of the theatrical convention where even a bad joke is better than none to relieve the monotony. Beckett uses the mechanism to expose the comically sad poverty of dialogue that accompanies the decay of flesh, mind and words.

That minimal dialogue is further eked out by a kind of *as if* dialogue: Winnie's play-long and compulsive calls to her silent and mostly invisible partner. From her first hailing 'Hoo-oo' to her final anxious appeal ('Have you gone off your head, Willie? (*Pause.*) Out of your poor old wits, Willie?'), there is hardly a page in the text where Winnie is not *speaking to* the silent partner. Willie's final spoken syllable – 'Win' – is the only actual reply in this long series of admonitions, questions and requests, comments and expostulations. The countlessly repeated *'you* -turn' in the texture of Winnie's speech transforms her soliloquy into outward-directed speech – and gives the 'story of a solitary person' theatrical dynamism.

The other theatrical devices in *Happy Days* are Winnie's stream of self-apostrophising remarks and her stories or impersonations. In addressing herself, Winnie is given a device often found in the traditional soliloquy (in *Hamlet.* for instance) where the introspective protagonist 'talks to himself', 'thinks aloud':

How often I have said, in evil hours, Sing now, Winnie, sing your song, there is nothing else for it, and did not [. . .] Something says, Stop talking now, Winnie, for a minute, don't squander all your words for the day, stop talking and do something for a change, will you? (p. 31)

Unlike the Elizabethan soliloquy and unlike Winnie's reflections on the status of the continuing self (p. 85 above), remarks like these have little philosophical or emotional pressure behind them. They are just part of the way the speech-automaton functions, exhibiting the simple switching on/off mechanism that triggers verbal action – speech or silence or song. Perception of that primitive function is potentially frightening (we recall the terror released by Lucky's shattered faculty of speech) but the naive simplicity of Winnie's way of talking to herself keeps up the smiling tone of her recitation – the ironic 'happy day' mood we had seen in so many features of the play.

Winnie's stories, however, introduce elements of violence and moments of horror. The first story, of Mildred and the mouse, (pp. 41, 44), is very effective locally in that it has both the feel of a tale told in the nursery (the 'off-with-his-head' type of fright) and a dramatic climax when Winnie enacts Mildred's scream as the mouse rushes up her nightgown. The sense of violation is direct and sensual. Even so, the relation of the story to the overall pattern of the play is not clear (it does not, I think, have the felt appropriateness of the story of how Hamm ignored the pleas of the starving child's father – images of cruelty that directly allude to Hamm as tyrant). One suspects that the Mildred story is related to some childhood sexual experience of Winnie's, but it would be unrewarding to embark on detailed psychological speculations around that possibility. It is enough to have the image of the frightened, screaming child – the experience of trauma – brought into the otherwise so carefully nurtured superficial optimism of Winnie's speech-flow.

The story of the Showers or Cookers – 'last human kind to stray this way' (p. 33) – has a crude theatrical energy. Winnie's impersonation of that vulgar couple of spectators suddenly forces the audience (which may have settled down to view Winnie as an acceptable static exhibit) to see her diminished body through voyeur eyes:

What's she doing? he says – What's the idea? he says – stuck up to her diddies in the bleeding ground – coarse fellow – What does it mean? he says – What's it meant to mean? – and so on. (Act I, p. 32)

Can't have been a bad bosom, he says, in its day. (*Pause.*) Seen worse shoulders, he says, in my time. (*Pause.*) Does she feel her legs? he says. (*Pause.*) Is there any life in her legs he says. (*Pause.*) Has she anything on underneath? he says. (*Pause.*) Ask her, he says, I'm shy. (*Pause.*) Ask her what? she says. (*Pause.*) Is there any life in her legs. (*Pause.*) Has she anything on underneath. (Act II, p. 43)

Over and above the immediate effect of jolting us into a new perspective as spectators, Winnie's improvisation of this scene again uses a device from the popular theatre (reminiscent of the music hall). The second scene is presented just as Winnie's classics are about to be exhausted – for the day. Mr Shower's crude observations are then brought in to help out when other words fail; in the stage direction to her appeal to Willie there is a long pause for thinking of *some* resource or other:

And now? (*Pause.*) And now, Willie? (*Long pause.*) I call to the eye of the mind . . . Mr Shower – or Cooker. (*She closes her eyes. Bell rings loudly. She opens her eyes. Pause.*) Hand in hand, in the other hands bags.(p. 43)

In places like this we witness how memory – that endless stream of words tending to soliloquy – is being dramatised. Here as elsewhere we note also the *rhythm* of the phrases and pauses, with the omnipresent stage directions as signals to a continuous performance. We might call that the *Happy Days* rhythm – highly characteristic and to be developed in the later plays. The text may at first be difficult to *read* because of the dominant use of so many short, staccato phrases interspersed with stage directions, marking the almost incessant pauses (see the passages quoted on pp. 81 and 85). It is like no play-text encountered before. But that difficulty is yet another indication that we are dealing with a markedly performance-directed dramatic score: the words are asking to be heard. Under conditions more extreme than the diminished theatre of *Waiting for Godot* and *Endgame*, something seemingly as 'undramatic' as the casual thoughts of a woman imprisoned in a decaying body is projected into a continuous speech-flow: it turns into a 'star performance', as if created out of the scattered remnants of a play.

6

Play

We have seen that each new Beckett play opens a new direction in response to a persistent urge to innovate. When *Play* was first produced in England (The National Theatre at the Old Vic, 1964), it had the immediate impact of a radically new work, with its three isolated speakers in their urns responding to the summons of a spotlight, rhythmically speaking at great speed, unintelligibly in the opening minutes. It seemed the ultimate diminishment of dramatic character, action and dialogue; at the same time, the stage image of those talking heads compelled immediate attention, as they were lit up one after the other for a brief interval of time. After the speakers began to spell out their 'story' in the first sequence (with rapid variations and overlapping points of view that hardly gave the audience time to unify the fragmented information), the second sequence clearly suggested that all three voices were speaking from some limbo beyond earthly life. The full replay of the sequences then reinforced and eked out the audience's partial understanding of the first round: completing a verbal puzzle as well as a musical pattern.

The passage of time since the play's first production has confirmed that *Play* is a new kind of play for Beckett: a deliberate reduction of stage figures to talking automata who nevertheless retain human emotions and relevance. Action is now fully abstracted from the arena of the world as we know it, in so far as that is possible in the medium of the theatre. Yet the immobile and breathless speakers recreate a minimal retrospective plot – of farcical / melodramatic adultery and inevitable suffering – as if enacting the compressed version of a cheap play. And new technical devices in the patterning of audio-visual and verbal effects are used to express, with great precision, a new field of Beckett's vision: aspects of an unromantic life-in-death, recorded as if on tape.

Beckett himself divided *Play* into Chorus, Narration and Meditation – a structural order that illuminates the remembered action and a subsequent vision. The Chorus immediately suggests a world 'elsewhere', with faint, barely comprehensible voices descanting on some theme of dark survival: 'Yes, strange, darkness best' / 'Yes, perhaps, a shade gone' / 'Yes, peace, one assumed' . . . They are speaking so faintly and quickly that only repetition, or a reading of the text, will allow an audience to connect those fragments into a text. The incantation of those toneless voices comes over like something half-heard yet insistent, an affirmative lament or sorrowful good news. The opening 'yes' is a unison of acceptance. After that W1 speaks of some unearthly space–time, present and future ('darkness, all dark, and the time to come'); W2 offers a cliché-type everyday acceptance ('I'm all right, still all right, do my best, all I can – '); and M appears to be rehearsing one of the speculative key motifs of *Play*, concerning the illusory nature of all experience: 'all out, all the pain, all as if . . . never been, it will come – '. It is a fallen chorus (in contrast to the chorus of Greek drama), which can only offer a pointer to its own shadowy setting, a place of diminution, an unspecific underworld. And it can only hint at some former state (W2's 'gone' M's 'never been'), a past that has a story to be conjured up from the shades, from the fragments of memory and language.

As if telling a story

The sequence of narration (pp. 10–15) plunges at once into sordid particulars of adultery and sexual jealousy. We hear brief extracts from a story the three speakers proceed to tell in such a way that the three series of information untimately converge, even though they diverge in timing. There is no unison; the sound effect is that of a round. And the narrative resembles the proceedings at an improperly conducted trial where three very partial witnesses compulsively respond to a silent prompter (the spotlight) trying to tell the truth – the partial truth. To this fusion of limited points of view – a technique of narration that has perhaps never been used in drama in such a radical way before – Beckett gives a twist. The telling itself becomes intensely tragicomic. For as the speakers are not allowed to tell their story either simultaneously or consecutively, the tale cannot unfold. It can only be presented as an oral mosaic. But the pieces of the mosaic are strongly coloured from the start, giving an immediate image of a marital crisis, with high-toned suspicions of infidelity:

[second speech of] W1: I said to him, Give her up. [. . .]
[second speech of] M: . . . Give up that whore, she said, or I'll cut my throat –
[third speech of] W2: Give up whom? I smell you off him, she screamed, he stinks of bitch.

The stages of this domestic drama then get established, fragment by fragment: after the accusations of infidelity offered by W1
(the wife, we assume) and the inevitable show-down scene between W1 and W2 (first reported by W2, ahead of the other two
speakers), we hear of M's confession (first from W1), followed by
W1 forgiving M and re-visiting W2 to offer gloating forgiveness
to her (first told by W2). But the affair continues in its banal round
'In the meantime we were to carry on as before', reports W2
(ahead of the other speakers), until it suddenly fizzles out, and all
three speakers are transported, unknown to each other, to the
hellish time and place they are currently occupying.

The story is, no doubt, deliberately banal, as often in Beckett,
to underscore the minimal experience that makes up the
characters' own drama. That effect is further intensified by the
marked presence of farcical and melodramatic language: conven-
tionally absurd elements of the pre-absurd theatre. The compression and speed of the story further minimises it, with the kind of
satirical perspective on a 'love affair' that Swift brought to
political and social affairs through the Lilliputians. And all these
levels of awareness are fused and sharpened by the audience's
early realisation that the speakers are speaking from a no-place
that gives the sordid particulars which are being recalled an unreal
sense of time, as if the past had not happened, or had happened
in a whirl that reduced willed and planned events to the level of
meaningless accidents. In the terms of traditional philosophy, they
recall events as mere contingency, lacking essential life. Their
utterances are part of a mechanism that looks automatic, as
elsewhere in Beckett, but here the focus is on the mechanism itself.

Voices in limbo

The long meditation gives a certain depth of feeling – and a certain universality – to the empty machination of the narrative.
The fragmentation of utterance – the staccato phrasing –
becomes more desperate as each of the characters tries to tell of
present experience, changing to the present tense – with faint
memories of the past, and still fainter imaginations of the future.
We can distinguish several overlapping threads in this tapestry of
brief statements:

1   meditations on the self, which repeatedly involve a questioning
    of the inquisitor: whoever operates that spotlight, inhuman
    and unidentifiable.

2 reflections on the limbo-like space in which the characters have been thrust suddenly and without explanation.

3 memories of, and speculations about, the others – springing from ignorance of their fate, laced with nostalgia, regrets and benevolent fantasies.

These motifs are intertwined and are thrown into the confessional pattern at random (a randomness that contrasts with the precision of the 'scoring', as we shall see). All three characters utter fragmentary statements, questions, and exclamations on the above three motifs, but with different kinds of emphasis and tone. On a second hearing (and in reading the text) these tonalities can just be distinguished within the rapid polyphonic chant of the ghost-speakers.

W1 seems to be the most spiritual among the three speakers, questioning her condition with a desperate urgency – perhaps the urgency of the damned still hoping for redemption, or at least for the cessation of pain. 'Mercy, mercy' is an appropriate opening cry. The expectation of something still *to come* (speech one) harmonises with the words spoken by W1 in the chorus, which foreshadows the metaphysical phrases in the meditation. W1 is clamorous in her ongoing contest with the powers that move the spotlight: 'Or you will weary of me. Get off me', (p. 15). She is pleading: 'I can do nothing . . . for anybody . . . any more . . . thank God. So it must be something I have to say. How the mind works still!' And she is questioning ironically, as if some act of penance might end the torture: 'Bite off my tongue and swallow it? Spit it out? Would that placate you? How the mind works still to be sure!' (p. 18).

This speaker's tragicomic intensity (the authentic Beckett voice) often evokes laughter from the audience: 'get off me', wrestling with the spotlight, sounds like wrestling with the incubus, with a clumsy lover. Then her speech modulates into Job-like arguments with a god who fails to do justice by one of his creatures. That is in keeping with W1 speaking in approximate theological terms concerning the limbo around her: 'Hellish half light' (pp. 16, 21), a phrase that recalls *Happy Days*; 'And that all is falling, all fallen, from the beginning, on empty air.' Given that intensity, that all-consuming interest in her present state of being, after what seemed like living, W1 has little energy left to meditate on her lover and her rival. For a second her old acrimony is revived ('She had means, I fancy, though she lived like a pig') only to give way to precisely worded fantasies ('Perhaps she has taken him away to live'), and vague benevolence: 'Poor creature. Poor creatures' (pp. 19–20). The speaker then returns to mystical meditations on the prayed-for silence and darkness (p. 21), probably the foremost consolation for being so diminished, in a state between life and death.

W2's utterances have a similar pattern of topics, but her vocabulary and tone are more down-to-earth and peremptory. She might as well be arguing with a 'real person', a false friend (someone like M) in her colloquial tussle with the unknown powers: 'Some day you will tire of me and go out . . . for good' (p. 16). Thus this speaker adds to the expectation of a dark apocalypse. But, in contrast to W1's spiritual anguish, we get a more urbane, sceptical shrugging off of the meaning of the universe: 'No doubt I make the same mistake as when it was the sun that shone, of looking for sense where possibly there is none' (p. 177). It is W2 who then expresses, in this abandoned place, the fear that she may not even be listened to or looked at (p. 17), a fear that is recurrent among Beckett characters from Vladimir on: a *felt* parallel to the position taken in Berkeley's idealist philosophy where existence depends on being perceived.

W2 also meditates about her rival: 'That poor creature' (p. 18), deliberately echoing one of W1's characteristic phrases ('I can hear her') *before* it is spoken in the text. Such cross-weaving is part of the complex verbal tapestry, as in the sequence that follows where W2's pity for the lovers overlaps with M pitying the two women (pp. 18–19). But her meditation ends on a note of self-examination: doubting her own sanity, but dismissing the doubt. This tone again presents a robust spirit in that twilight world.

Into the counterpoint of these two female voices is scored M's distinctive male and worldly voice. M tends to have the lightest style among the three speakers, with occasional comic bathos, as when he contemplates the present torture against the hoped-for final silence thus: 'It will come. Must come. There is no future in this' (p. 16). On the other hand, repeating and developing his motif from the Chorus (see pp. 92–3, 98) it is M who is once more brooding on his past life as a theatrical illusion followed by the present state which will likewise turn into 'just play':

I know now, all that was just . . . play. And all this? When will all this – [W1 and W2 interrupt as if mocking M]: 'All this, when will all this have been . . . just play. (pp. 16–17)

M is also the speaker who is given the most fully embodied nostalgia for his spoilt love affair, with a sentimental fantasy, an idyll for three: 'Never woke together, on a May morning, the first to wake the other two' (p. 20). M's all-too-human sentimentality, balanced by an interest in the world's mundane's sights and tastes (his preference for Lipton's tea), and his self-interrupting hiccups, provides another comic element in *Play*.

Language, rhythm and theatre

Play is sombre but not solemn – a fusion of a Dantesque under-world and a tragicomic puppet play. The three speakers are sometimes seen and heard as representative characters recording experiences, expressing suffering; then, at a switch of the light, or while one of them is still speaking, they are perceived to be robot-like reciters of 'their' actions and feelings. The idiom of these pseudo-characters is also a blend of all kinds of stage-talk, from the naturalistic to the highly literary. Either of these styles can sound comic, and doubly comic when spoken in the same context by the same speakers:

W1: And there was no denying he continued as . . . assiduous as ever.
This, and his horror of the merely Platonic thing, made me
sometimes wonder if I were not accusing him unjustly. Yes.
(p. 11)

W1: Just a common tart. What he could have found in her when he had
me –   (p. 13)

The repeated juxtaposition of stilted literary phrases and the slangy clichés of a marital soap opera, has an insidious liveliness about it. But since all the phrases are spoken in a toneless and accelerated voice, in a kind of posthumous gabble, the liveliness has a 'canned' effect too, replayed like a tape recording at unnatural speed.

The vocal impact is governed by the insistent staccato rhythm. It is a carefully designed musical/verbal pattern which nevertheless creates the effect of random bursts of speech activity – on and off, alert and dead. The whole play is an aural tapestry (which is not to minimise the visual impact in the theatre). Beckett himself provides a precise notation for the speech rhythms of the Chorus which opens the play:

W1:	Yes strange	darkness best	and the darker	the worse
W2:	Yes perhaps	a shade gone	I suppose	some might say
M :	Yes peace	one assumed	all out	all the pain

W1:	till all dark	then all well	for the time	but it will come
W2:	poor thing	a shade gone	just a shade	in the head
M :	all as if	never been	it will	come *hiccup* pardon

(p. 23)

The Narrative and the Meditation are to be spoken in less stylised, less breathless and more varied rhythms – in keeping with the stylistic variation just indicated. But the three voices share the dominant staccato rhythm – like gasps, as if the language as well as the speakers were getting short of breath – throughout the play. Even before the words are distinctly heard or grasped, this insistent rhythm conveys 'fundamental sounds' – less than human, automatic and macabre. It is a rhythm that Beckett is to use repeatedly in the later monologues, and one can see why: it amounts to dramatisation of the inner voices of thought, that is, fragments of thoughts emerging out of solipsistic isolation, as if at the bidding of a cruel task-master. Lucky's speech was probably the first version of this automatic rhythm; but the voices in *Play* are not pathological, only disembodied, or in the process of getting disembodied.

That rhythm, appropriately enough, makes us aware of the physical foundations of speech – the effort of forming sounds with the organs of speech, lips, tongue, teeth, above all breathing. Breath has to be gathered for each new burst of word-formation within the larger effort of joining up sounds and words, an effort never quite successful because constantly interrupted by the spotlight. One is reminded of the importance attached to breath and breathing as a primary human activity by Beckett. His minimal play *Breath* is 'about' just that. (This corresponds to the original connection between the meaning of the words *breath* and *spirit* and, in our own time, the importance attached to breathing by certain poets, for instance by Allan Ginsberg.)

The extent to which Beckett wishes to control the progression of speed and volume within the overall rhythm of performance can be seen, in addition to the stage directions, in the instructions recorded by Martin Esslin on the occasion of an experimental radio production of *Play* (*Encounter*, September 1975, p. 44). In these instructions an elaborate arithmetic of rhythmic variations is worked out according to which 'each subsection [in the text] is both faster and softer than the preceding one. If the speed of the first Chorus is 1 and its volume 1, then the speed of the first Narration must be 1 plus 5 per cent and its volume 1 minus 5 per cent. The speed of the following segment, the first Meditation, must then be (1 plus 5 per cent) plus 5 per cent, and its volume (1 minus 5 per cent) minus 5 per cent.' And so on, the text to go on *ad infinitum*. It is the furthest move in Beckett's drama so far towards linguistic abstraction, far from the approximate dialogue of Beckett's early plays, the give-and-take encounter of the paired couples in *Waiting for Godot* and *Endgame*.

The device of the spotlight as a non-human inquisitor and prompter seems equally radical and successful. It immediately fuses two strongly physical images: that of the stage and of the modern torture chamber. (People in the audience will recall the notorious method of secret police interrogation under a powerful electric light.) The spotlight remains utterly unreachable, thereby condemning the three speakers to isolation: they are to remain monologuists and speech automata in relation to their questioner, in addition to remaining sealed off from one another in a triangular array of monologues. No wonder each speaker in turn is engaged in a struggle, fitfully titanic but dwarfed inevitably, against the relentless impact of the spotlight. Beckett has given a great deal of attention to the synchronisation of light and sound, with the rhythm of light dictating the rhythm of sound. Some productions follow Beckett's suggestion (made in the course of a rehearsal) that the light should fade, with the voices fading or pausing longer before each new summons. But whatever the exact rhythm, the sense of talking automata dominates, strengthened by the revised stage direction: 'The response to light is immediate' (originally: 'the response to light is not quite immediate').

The puppet speakers do, however, appear to engage in a kind of conversation mainly through the accidental juxtaposition of phrases spoken – in isolation – by the separate speakers, for example:

M: So I told her I did not know what she was talking about.
Spot from M to W2.
W2: What are you talking about? (p. 10)

Similar cross-weavings occur throughout the text: an echoing of words and phrases, seemingly telling the same story from different angles (as in the examples given above: 'give up' and 'pity', p. 93 and 96 respectively). It is as if the speakers compensated for their total isolation through a kind of 'verbal telepathy' that binds them together (to borrow a phrase from the critic Alec Reid). So we have the paradox of Beckett's seemingly most abstract monologuists contributing to verbal patterns that often sound like dialogue. The audience becomes aware of this device – an illusion of interaction between separated body–minds – during the repetition of the play, if not earlier.

The repetition is a complete replay, in this respect out-doing one of Krapp's tapes, but here there is no intelligent, questioning controller, only the merciless spotlight just discussed. The replay not only helps the audience to work out the patterns and meaning of the whole play (a necessary device in the performance of certain compressed pieces of modern music), but also reinforces the overall impression of infinite rotation. Beckett wanted to suggest such infinity in earlier plays – in *Waiting for Godot* and in *Happy Days* – with their patterns of cyclic repetition in two acts. However, both of those plays had variations in the pattern woven into the repetition, and a certain openness in the ending (as in the second appearance of the Boy *in Waiting for Godot*.) Only in *Play* is the repetition exact, unvaried and palpably beyond the grasp and control of any character. An infinite series of repetitions is easy to imagine. But artistically one re-play is enough to establish the correspondence between a particular vision of life and a particular medium – between the endless rotation of human actions and voices and a theatre of audio-visual effects that makes the mechanism of such a rotation felt on the pulses of the audience. The erotic dance of three just visible persons is performed as puppetry, in a specially created theatre for talking marionettes.

II
THE TRILOGY OF NOVELS

7

Contexts for the fiction

Beckett's novels are radically innovative, yet they grow out of, or lean against, certain traditions of fictional writing. Among these is the tradition that parodies the act of writing a novel itself, initiated, in many provocatively funny variations, in Sterne's *Tristram Shandy* (1760–7). In that mode of fiction the writer is for ever conscious of himself and of writing – the empty sheet on the table, the silence, the compulsion to invent, 'to lie', the physical act of wielding pen or pencil (no other writing implements in Beckett). And the 'story' being told is simultaneously seen as an artifact being shaped, here and now: open-ended in many potential directions yet tediously bound by the teller's labour. Frequently, especially in *Molloy*, remnants of the once-strong picaresque novel are fused with this self-conscious fictionalising: a journey with adventures, chance digressions, inner stories and authorial commentaries filling in the fictional space. The outcasts, the bums, the cripples and the sad wretches that people Beckett's world of fiction are 'at home' on the abandoned road, in the ditch, on the sick-bed, and perhaps unimaginable in the social contexts of realist/empiricist fiction.

Along with the novel-parodying mode goes a savagely ironic self-inspecting narrator. Aware of the decay of (his) body–mind and its functions, this narrator (elegiac when not satirical, accompanied by Swiftian savage laughter) presents a ceaseless commentary on his non-well-being. His existential perplexities – about his present and past state of being and experiencing – are at least as significant as the 'story' he sets out to tell. The voice of this doubting and self-ironising self fuses with the voice of the narrator reflecting on the parodied act of writing. These two voices – two levels of self-consciousness – thus present two kinds of 'meta-narration' or narratives beyond the supposed core 'story' in the fabric of the novel.

The doubting self enriches the parody-novel with variations on some of the main themes of Western philosophical meditation. A stream of reiterated questions revolves around the central, obsessively self-revealing narrator-character: why exist at all? how can I know myself, let alone things, persons, occurrences? Meditation on such questions of being and knowledge – traditional ontology and epistemology – is embedded in the 'showing' of the self. The 'philosophising' is only an aspect of the existentially experienced frailty and fret. The attentive reader can participate in this aspect of the quest without necessarily tracking down the questions to Beckett's principal sources: the supposed split between the physical/mechanical and the mental/spiritual universes (Descartes, 1596–1650, and his followers, especially Geulincx, 1624–69, best remembered for his 'Where you are worth nothing, there you should want nothing');[1] and the assumption that there is no reality except in the mind (Berkeley, 1685–1753). (See also Introduction pp. 3, 9–10.)

Such traditional literary and philosophical elements are used by Beckett to give the novel a wholly new direction, distinct from the approach of any of the three great modernist writers – Proust, Joyce and Kafka – with whom Beckett has an affinity. Proust in his *Remembrance of Things Past* (1913–27) is preoccupied with the rich tapestry of upper-class social interaction as well as with the psychological subtleties of Marcel's mind; it is Beckett's art that increasingly approaches the X-ray negative. (The 'radiographic' image was applied by Beckett to Proust, see Introduction, pp. 8–9, 12–13). Moreover, Proust's novel cycle leads towards discovery – memory and art as ways of redeeming time; Beckett's novels end with failure or death, though the trilogy ends, in *The Unnamable*, with the supreme paradox: 'I can't go on, I'll go on.' Joyce (see Introduction pp. 8, 11–12) worked towards a gigantic and punning novel-universe that would ultimately embrace the whole gamut of outer and inner reality. By contrast, Beckett works towards simplification and exclusion – towards 'lessness'. Beckett shares Joyce's intense obsession with language, and his earlier fiction – including *Murphy* – shows a style loaded with local parody and mannerism; but, in the developing trilogy and later fiction, the words get leaner, the verbal experimentation is pared down. And while Joyce pondered every word, like Flaubert, Beckett has claimed: 'I don't know where the writing comes from and I am often quite surprised when I see what I have committed to paper. Writing, for me, is an entirely different process than it was for Joyce.'[2] Finally, Beckett goes much further than Kafka in creating fictional uncertainty in and for his narratives, beyond the existential uncertainty of a character. Kafka tends to build chapters causally and chronologically, while Beckett undermines the structure of time itself. Beckett himself is said to have considered Kafka classical and 'almost serene'. The Kafka world's terrors – the sudden inexplicable threat and the arbitrary summons, in a quasi-religious allegory – are pushed in Beckett's fiction towards disintegration, in black comedy.

The comedy is not just one thread in fables predominantly concerned with human failure and suffering; it is as fully integrated in the narrative as the tragicomic action is in the structure of the plays. However, it is unevenly spread across the trilogy: *Molloy* (especially part one) may well rank among the great comic novels, among other things; but the comedy, like everything else, diminishes by the time we reach the broken voice of *The Unnamable*, and with the decline of comedy there is a decline in readability too. This is partly because the very form and texture of the novels embody the cycle of decline – a pattern of continuous regression. As the narrator's body and mind diminish, so the resources of *writing* diminish too. This is graphically shown in the ending of *Malone Dies* where the narrator's constantly diminishing pencil and consciousness finally peter out, on the threshold of death, in a final paralysis of the writer's mind and hand:

> or with it or with his hammer or with his stick or with
> his fist or in thought in dream I mean never he will
> never
>
> or with his pencil or with his stick or
>
> or light light I mean
>
> never there he will never
>
> never anything
>
> there
>
> any more

Beckett's novel becomes a metaphor for its subject, the form and the language 'imitating' what is narrated. Here, too, the approach is different from Joyce. Whilst Joyce – in *Ulysses* – creates a specific fictional language for each character (a dramatic language that does 'imitate' the character's condition, with the narrator withdrawing), Beckett's novels tend to be dominated by the omnipresent though impotent narrator. That self-telling narrator has a variety of voices or styles, and a shifting consciousness, but he cannot create a character, a voice, a style wholly distinct from himself; or he can do so only with the greatest difficulty (a difficulty that becomes part of the narratorial self-mockery). What the narratorial voice expresses or 'imitates' recurrently is, above all, its own gradual diminishment. As in *Waiting for Godot* and the later plays, the slow, inexorable deterioration of the self (body and mind decaying in parallel states, it would seem) is the controlling vision of the novels – both individually and taken together. Thus the trilogy as a whole can be seen to present a cycle of diminishment: moving, roughly, from the broad, mock-heroic quest-novel, *Molloy*, to the broken memoir of a dying man in *Malone Dies*, and so to the confessional of a self that can find no self of any substance in *The Unnamable*. But this should not be seen as a scheme, a premeditated cycle like the decline of the generations in a realistic family saga (for instance in Thomas Mann's *Buddenbrooks*). There is no evidence that Beckett had a detailed plan for the trilogy, even though the idea of three narrations is mentioned early in the English version of *Molloy*:

> This time, then once more I think, then perhaps a last time, then I think it'll be over, with that world too. (p. 2)

The trilogy probably developed gradually, from a germinal idea, into something like a pilgrim's regress – each novel carrying a central preoccupation with being and diminishment further and further. It follows that the three novels are very different in texture and that each can be read separately as a complete novel, even though they are best read as parts of one major work. Repetition of phrases (motifs) and internal cross-references abound; Beckett's self-conscious narrators themselves refer to each other from time to time. *Molloy* is probably the best entry into Beckett's longer fiction though it was his fifth novel, preceded, among others,[3] by the exhilarating *Murphy* (1938).

Murphy, Beckett's only English novel to be published before the Second World War, has not yet broken with third-person narration and some of the conventions of the comic novel fused with the *Bildungsroman*, tracing the hero's intellectual progress and adventures. Several keynotes of Beckett's fiction are sounded in *Murphy* in an immediately accessible and hilariously comic mode. The hero devotes most of his energy, or lethargy, to finding ways of avoiding work in a life of total self-delighting solitude, rocking in his rocking chair, held in position by seven scarves – no guarantee against the rocking chair toppling over. Murphy is, like other Beckett anti-heroes, a 'seedy solipsist', whose isolation is both actual and philosophical. His life, or what is left of living, cannot connect mind and body, and cannot reconcile his need of 'self-immersed indifference to the contingencies of the contingent world' with his passion for Celia (a one-time prostitute and the one character in the novel whose body and soul cohere). Of course, to couple a determined solipsist with a 'normal', world-loving, sexual partner is in itself a fine comic invention. The reliance on incongruity and 'intrigue' are also marks of the traditional comic novel. And the hero has some traditional novelistic features too: far from being isolated in a timeless/nameless world – the direction in Beckett's later fiction – he is pursued by lovers and well-wishers; the time is marked with total precision (the days of the month in the year of 1936 are needed to prepare Murphy's horoscope, chapter 3); and the novel's topography of London and Dublin can be checked on the relevant street maps.

Such an approach is partly a parody of all those familiar details – the verisimilitude and verifiability – nurtured by the realistic novel. So Celia is introduced (in chapter 2) by listing her 'vital statistics' down to the sizes of her knee, calf and ankle. But it is also a sign that we are reading Beckett's early fiction: 'the big world' Murphy wants to escape from is still circumstantially present, if only through parody and pastiche. There is even a consistent-seeming if inconsequential comic plot involving the quartet of Dublin characters who are pursuing Murphy – Neary, Wylie, Cooper and Miss Counihan, who is still in love with Murphy in hiding – stage Irish caricatures, speaking in highly mannered, often mock-erudite language. Even the phases of Murphy's self-chosen retreat into the Magdalen Mental Mercyseat (as a male nurse) and his gruesome end in that institution are presented robustly, that is to say 'absurdly' in the old pre-absurdist sense of grotesque and comic action. His experiment in self-isolation ends in a broadly tragicomic catastrophe (Murphy is literally exploded, having pulled the wrong lavatory chain, a Heath Robinsonish contraption that releases gas instead of water). After the cremation, Murphy's ashes are scattered, by mistake, on the floor of a saloon bar, and 'swept away with the sand, the beer, the butts, the glass, the matches, the spits, the vomit' (chapter 13).

In sum, it is not yet the novel *of* the totally isolated self, for not only is Murphy moving in a peopled galaxy, but the third-person narrative is kept at a considerable move from the complex confessional monologue that is to make up the texture of the trilogy. Murphy's alienation – in the mental hospital – is presented through explicit narratorial commentary: we are told of his sympathy with the patients, and his loathing for 'the textbook attitude towards them, the complacent scientific conceptualism that made contact with outer reality the index of mental well-being' (chapter 9). The language has, so to speak, not yet fallen. The reader is not yet directly exposed to the abnormalities of Murphy's speech, but is *told* about his speech by the omniscient novelist via Celia's observation: 'She felt, as she felt so often with Murphy, spattered with words that went dead as soon as they sounded; each word obliterated, before it had time to make sense, by the word that came next; so that in the end she did not know what had been said. It was like difficult music heard for the first time' (end of chapter 3). The feeling of direct immersion, in a wholly verbal universe gone wrong, is still to be created – in the trilogy, where all experience is filtered through or refracted by the words of the first-person narrator's diminishing self.

8

Molloy

The quest

We focus first on the epic sweep of Molloy's quest in part one of this novel: with its hilarious and horrifying digressions (the picaresque), its random but ultimately linked speculative questions (the philosophical novel), its parodic humour and lyrical pathos (remnants of 'the old style'). True, the context of the whole work, indeed of the whole trilogy, is needed for its proper appreciation, especially of its narrative design – parallels and variations – but this context may be postponed for the moment.

Molloy's quest for his mother is one of Beckett's best-sustained narrative units, which can be read – ideally read aloud – with a delighted sense of immediacy. For there is nothing 'slow', in novelistic terms, about the laborious, halting, often arrested, and finally crawling movements of this half-senile cripple. His journey is doomed to seem interminable and futile, but his report on the journey (the self-conscious fiction) has a tone of despairing exhilaration. Molloy as narrator is 'informative' from the start; he may be an ignorant, agnostic or unreliable reporter, but he is not grudging with presentation of the self. He is not secretive, nor, given his limitations, obscure. His initial situation is presented with the forthrightness of a Robinson Crusoe: he is stranded in his mother's room, confined and *obliged* to tell of past adventures, of the long road to that room by his former self, before he had reached his present decrepitude: 'What I'd like now is to speak of the things that are left, say my good-byes, finish dying' (p. 1).

His quest is to reach his mother, a purpose sustained to the end of Part One. That quest is a narrative thread on which all the lesser journeys are hung, with frequent reminders of the elusive goal, amid all the other episodes and meditations, as in a classic odyssey. And it is worth noting that this quest carries conviction – at least in the terms of Molloy's report – whether or not it is judged sane. It is like Don Quixote's obsessive search for the vanished age of chivalry or Captain Ahab's hunting of the white whale; indeed it is more 'reasonable', given the centrality of the mother figure in our culture. A primal obsession is consistently conveyed through this search. It is driven by Molloy's emotional ambivalence towards his mother: his grotesquely inflamed disgust mingling with the wish to be reunited with her. In his attitude to other people Molloy similarly swings from misanthropic solitariness to longing for companionship, as in the early encounter with A and C (see below, pp. 122–3). Molloy's paradoxical desire for loathed company is as interesting as the journey itself: the indefatigable efforts of a weary man to reach an unattainable goal. This underlying emotional pattern gradually emerges, without calling for a psychoanalytic interpretation.

The mother motif is first sounded as a 'high theme' with a deliberate Christian resonance (which we note without regarding it as a governing symbol):

But talking of the craving for a fellow let me observe that having waked between eleven o'clock and midday (I heard the angelus [the bell], recalling the incarnation, shortly after) I resolved to go and see my mother. I needed, before I could resolve to go and see that woman, reasons of an urgent nature, and with such reasons, since I did not know what to do, or where to go, it was child's play for me, the play of an only child, to fill my mind until it was rid of all other preoccupation and I seized with a trembling at the mere idea of being hindered from going there, I mean to my mother, there and then.   (p. 16)

We find here traditional reverence and an urgency of emotion deliberately mimed, that is, chosen but also faked. There is also uncertainty and lack of purpose: 'since I did not know what to do' . . . But, within two pages, the 'high theme' of the mother figure is put down into a 'low theme' presenting, with grotesque satirical concreteness, a 'deaf, blind, impotent, mad old woman', incontinent and making the room smell of ammonia, 'jabbering away with a rattle of dentures', to be knocked on the skull by Molloy as his only way of communicating with her – a memorable example of Beckett's imagery of decaying flesh (more savage than Swift). Passages like this usually mock the possibility of love towards, and physical contact with, another person. Molloy's resentment of his mother is traced back to the primal failure: being born at all ('the sin of having been born' – *Proust*, p. 67), and the mother's failure to prevent his existence. (Compare the biblical 'Why died I not from the womb?' (*The Book of Job* 3:11), and Hamm damning Nagg as his 'accursed progenitor' in *Endgame* (see chapter 2, pp. 51, 59).) Molloy's rage against his mother later shifts into his moments of misogynic contempt for the two loving women of the 'romance' sequence (Lousse and Ruth); these two merge into each other, and in turn merge into the figure of the mother, in recall. To give sexual pathology its due, male and female merge into androgynous figures, and there is no clear distinction in Molloy's memory between the rectum and the vagina. Such confusions help to turn Molloy – mythic yet physical – into the most concrete, fleshed out character in the trilogy. The novel gains from this concreteness – fusing a pathological case history with vivid fantasy. The monologue is tied to an embodied and conspicuously present narrator-hero. Thus Molloy can be visualised (and has indeed been successfully dramatised) as a repulsively attractive figure, while the later soliloquisers retreat into ever more spectral states.

All the other episodes in Molloy's report may be secondary from the point of view of the proclaimed quest for the mother, yet even minor episodes often loom large locally, emphasised by fictional space and fine writing. Clearly, Beckett has not written a plotted novel with themes carefully edited according to their significance and relation to each other – the novel is a continuous medley, with constant improvisation and parody (again the line from Sterne's *Tristram Shandy*). However, the reader and the critic need a grid of levels to keep track of the narrative episodes as well as the stream of meditations which flow across them, as Molloy's quest for self-knowledge gains in significance.

The succession of more or less external/physical episodes come nearest to the obstacles and enchantments found in the old picaresque novel, and make up the most dramatic sections of the comedy. (Yet even here we keep our ideas of anything happening physically 'out there' in inverted commas, knowing that we are reading a fictional record of mythologised memories.) No sooner has Molloy set out on his journey, with his crutches fastened to the crossbar of his bicycle, than he is arrested by an officious police sergeant from resting on his bicycle in a peculiar way. He comes under further suspicion – legitimately so from a bureaucratic point of view – for not being able to remember either his own or his mother's name, and for offering, instead of his identity papers, newspapers used as toilet paper (pp. 21 ff.). We may find in an episode like this a felicitous mixing of Fielding (Tom Jones arrested on false suspicion of thieving) and of Kafka (the arbitrary summons). Molloy next passes through a pastoral landscape, congratulating himself on being able to recognise, amid so much uncertainty, a shepherd and his dog and 'the anxious bleating' of the sheep (pp. 30 ff.). (Most pastoral scenes in the trilogy suggest

pre-industrial Ireland.) The short episode repays close reading to
see how the layers in the narrative are composed: with rapid, and
always unparagraphed, shifts from the pastoral to the meditative
(are all those sheep to be taken to the shambles?, etc.) to another
compulsive reminder of the first quest – 'to get to my mother'.
Molloy, distracted by a mock-heroic reflection on the seasons and
on his own chameleon-like needs, reminisces about his days as a
literary tramp (cf. Didi in *Godot*) who in winter used to wrap
himself in swathes of *The Times Literary Supplement*, found peculiarly
resistant to farts. A brief calculation of these compels a place in
Molloy's report (with an author's error in the arithmetic!).

Such ribald humour often ushers in searching self-examination
– in that quest for the self which becomes more explicit in the
course of narration. We see this quest through the sudden flashes
of a searchlight – sudden illumination – as distinct from the
more or less systematic self-analysis found in earlier realist and
modernist fiction (including Proust). The minimal story is then
the context – or the pretext – for that search for the inner self.
This is true even of the longest, seemingly epic, episode: Molloy's
stay in the house of Lousse (pp. 37–62), the nearest thing to a
parodied chapter from traditional romance literature, with Molloy
as the wanderer who becomes the half-willing, half-enchanted
server of his Lady. But any stricter interpretation along these
lines, with Lousse as the enchantress (like Homer's Circe) and
Molloy as the deformed lover, would soon fade out. It would have
to give way to the realisation that such traditional themes or motifs
are lightly sounded only to become the vehicle for more urgent
digressions on Molloy's bodily and mental states: his testicles, his
clothes, his other possessions (especially his bicycle which had
vanished) and, above all, his fears, his timid and finally determined
efforts to get away from the unwanted attentions of Lousse and her
grand household.

These earthly reports mingle with mystical insights, in privileged
moments of being. It is in the garden of Lousse, but not through
the ministrations of her person, that Molloy experiences serenity,
or the silence of the self. (Reporting on such an experience is a
recurrent 'positive' motif in the trilogy):

And there was another noise, that of my life become the life of this garden
as it rode the earth of deeps and wildernesses. Yes, there were times when
I forgot not only who I was, but that I was, forgot to be. Then I was no
longer that sealed jar to which I owed my being so well preserved, but a
wall gave way and I filled with roots and tame stems for example, stakes

long since dead and ready for burning, the recess of night and the imminence of dawn . . .   (pp. 51–2)

The image of the sealed jar for the self foreshadows the location of the suffering 'I'-voice in *The Unnamable* and can also remind us of the dominant elegiac mode of so many statements about the self in the Lousse episode and after:

And in the midst of those men I drifted like a dead leaf on springs, or else I lay down on the ground, and then they stepped gingerly over me as though I had been a bed of rare flowers.   (p. 55)

For my waking was a kind of sleeping . . . If I go on long enough calling that my life I'll end up by believing it. It's the principle of advertising. This period of my life. It reminds me, when I think of it, of air in a water-pipe.   (p. 56)

Molloy's exit from the domain of Lousse turns him into an even more solitary wanderer than before, dispossessed of all posses-sions. No longer belonging to anyone, he moves across an increas-ingly unrecognisable and unnamable landscape. With no bicycle, only his crutches to propel him, he moves ever more slowly, increasingly weak and handicapped, – in the pattern of diminish-ment which we have discerned in all the plays.

With the quest for the self now sounded with increasing urgency (though the quest for the mother remains the subject of recurrent allusion), major discoveries take Molloy to states of mind approx-imating non-self, or at least a state of minimal being and having and knowing – a movement towards less and less. Such a state repeatedly generates a fleeting rapture, comparable to the experience of self-forgetfulness already quoted. Soon after having left the gardens of Lousse, the contemplation of a silver object stolen from Lousse (see below, p. 123), leads Molloy to discover the peace of *not knowing*:

For to know nothing is nothing, not to want to know anything likewise, but to be beyond knowing anything, to know you are beyond knowing anything, that is when peace enters in, to the soul of the incurious seeker.   (p. 68)

That insight – with parallels in both Eastern and Western mysticism – is immediately followed by an ecstatic account of Molloy wielding his crutches, in 'a series of little flights, skimming the ground'. The two longer episodes which take Molloy first to the seaside (dwelling in a cave like Plato's learner–philosopher) and then through a thick forest (like Dante at the opening of the

Divine Comedy), abound in passages of serene insight – despite, or rather along with, the eloquently voiced despair ('a veritable calvary with no limits to its station and no hope of crucifixion' (p. 83) is the image evoked by the pain of having to walk on worsening legs). Other images of self-discovery accompany Molloy's ever-worsening condition in these final stages of the journey, until his legs finally give way and he is forced to 'abandon erect motion, that of man' (p. 94). The final sequence – as he crawls out of the forest towards the light, ending in a ditch – marks the failure of the whole quest. For his eyes are opened only to the realisation that he cannot recognise anything, town or field, still less the domain of his mother. But once more there is an upbeat counterpoint: Molloy's serenity, presented in lyrical prose. He can hear the promptings of an unidentified voice: 'Don't fret, Molloy, we're coming.' But his final state, like that of the two seekers in *Waiting for Godot*, is immobility.

The pattern of the concluding report – drawing on archetypal images like those associated with the painful journey through the forest, ending in a ditch – is the kind of universal or mythic narrative to which our response is, on one level, immediate. But the narrative need not (should not) be clinched as a transparent allegory – a kind of Pilgrim's Regress where every detail has a precise correspondence to a namable spiritual state. The conclusion does clarify the overall narrative of part one of the novel, especially the pathos of a quest with diminishing faculties and purpose. But the meaning of the novel remains open-ended, with further levels of narrative complexity, which cannot be discussed before we have read and interpreted the report of Molloy's supposed rescuer, Moran.

The quest for the quester

The second part of *Molloy* opens with puzzling simplicity. We now have a robust narrator, the directly self-introduced Jacques Moran, who tells us in pedantic detail about his circumstances – his house and household, his young son (also called Jacques and subjected to the rigours of a near-Victorian paternal discipline), his props, Martha the maid and Father Ambrose the priest, his conventional habits allied to an obsessively regular daily regime, and distinctly old-world ideas and prejudices. Even his solitude appears quite comfortable, relieved by that stable environment, periodic masturbation, and a fondness for hens and bees. All this we are told by a confident-sounding voice, in precise, 'logical', and neatly paragraphed prose. We tend to think that 'the affair is banal' (the words Moran himself uses about 'the Molloy affair', p. 106) – in complete contrast to the mysterious opening sequences of Part One of the novel. And we may ask: why is he telling us all this? What is the bearing of these domestic details on the one unexplained event: the unspecified instructions to Moran? These are read to him from a notebook (a poor man's annunciation?) by the thirsty and not particularly angel-like messenger Gaber (Gabriel?) representing a not particularly divine 'vast organisation' with a far from awesome chief, one Youdi (Judah? Jehovah?) pp. 100–2, 114–16). That may sound like something out of a detective story with religious overtones, what Graham Greene calls an 'entertainment'? (pp. 101–2, 114–16).

It is only later, nearly twenty pages into Moran's report, that the narrative gets more intense – both in its subject and in the way it is told. Then we take full note of Moran's early sense of crisis, even fatality (on first receiving the order 'to see about Molloy'): 'I am done for. My son too' (p. 99) . . . 'In such surroundings slipped away my last moments of peace and happiness' (p. 100). Under a 'calamitous' sky he later becomes aware that his life was 'running out, I knew not through what breach' (p. 110). These forebodings point to *his* quest or obscure mission, brooded on during a siesta when – in the darkness, lying between the sheets – Moran has a difficult spiritual struggle trying to clarify the images that haunt him (pp. 118–22). In the solitude and darkness, protected from the external world's 'spray of phenomena', Moran first meditates on the figure of an unnamed *him* 'who has need of me to be delivered, who cannot deliver myself' (p. 119). Tentatively, various images of Molloy emerge, accompanied by Moran's struggle to prepare himself for his obscure mission, to 'venture to consider the work I had on hand':

For where Molloy could not be, nor Moran either for that matter, there Moran could bend over Molloy.   (p. 119)

That sudden evocation of Molloy suggests a shadowy figure that can be reached only through silent concentration, through the imagination (resembling the creative act of an author 'bending over' a character not yet realised – see below, p. 120). In the process of imagining Molloy, Moran is beginning to change: his solitude deepens, and he assumes an affinity with Molloy, 'a kind of connection, and one not necessarily false'. The figure of Molloy is (in a conditional phrase, for all these images are provisional, inchoate) invested 'with the air of a fabulous being' – whom the reader may link with the mythic dimension of Molloy in Part One of the novel.

That mythic Molloy is strange and remote from Moran's world and yet his own private Molloy: 'Perhaps I had invented him, I mean found him ready-made in my head' (p. 120). The many attributes of 'the fabulous being' seem to be taken, among other things, from the lore of monsters and angels, overlapping presences that threaten and invite:

He panted. He had only to rise up within me for me to be filled with panting . . .
He rolled his head, uttering incomprehensible words.
He was massive and hulking, to the point of misshapenness. And without being black, of a dark colour . . .
This was how he came to me, at long intervals. Then I was nothing but uproar, bulk, rage, suffocation, effort unceasing, frenzied and vain. *Just the opposite of myself*, in fact. It was a change. And when I saw him disappear, his whole body a vociferation, I was almost sorry.
What it was all about I had not the slightest idea.

(pp. 121–2, emphasis added)

At that point we are beginning to see that Moran has found a disturbing counter-image of himself in this 'fabulous' Molloy: an aspect of his self that is also the opposite of his present self or persona: the over-rational, domesticated, meticulous Moran, whose voice dominates large parts of the narrative. There could be a conflict between this inward and mythic Molloy (and Moran's caricature of it), and the other Molloys listed (p. 123): the Molloy so inadequately described by Gaber in his orders, and 'the man of flesh and blood somewhere awaiting me'. The investigator having no clue about the 'real identity' of the person he is to stalk – 'What it was all about I had not the slightest idea' – works as a testing paradox on the modest detective story level. It works more powerfully on the symbolic level, where a figure that has multiple and ambivalent attributes, and whose 'real presence' cannot be defined or deciphered (even his name is not distinctly heard in the poor acoustics of the soul, p. 121), suggests a call that must be answered before it is understood. In our reading, this works both on the existential/religious plane (where Moran's private Molloy becomes instrumental in the release of a darkly conscious energy within himself), and on the narratorial plane (where the shadowy and many-shaped Molloy slowly coming into light is paralleled by the author/narrator's search for a character, other than himself). Both these directions play a part in the rest of the Moran narrative: the simple-minded bourgeois agent is gradually transformed into a thoughtful and suffering person, and so into a more resourceful, but also more disposessed, writer/fabulator (see also below, pp. 119ff.).

Moran's uncertainties about the nature of his mission (the inadequacy of Gaber's instructions is repeatedly mentioned, pp. 146, 156, 159) are underlined by his long delays: days of lingering preparation and domestic distraction – eighteen pages of narrative – pass between the sounding of a gong (like the gong heard by Molloy in the forest, p. 124 cf. p. 95) and his entry into the country of Molloy. Such devices of procrastination are needed by Moran to face a journey whose purpose is not known, and a terrifying inward journey towards his dark self. So Moran – 'making ready to go without knowing where he was going' (p. 133) – wanders around his house in a virtual rite of departure, exhibiting the good citizen's love of possessions with ambivalent caring and clinging: 'my trees, my bushes, my flower-beds, my tiny lawns, I used to think I loved them' (p. 137).

The Molloy country (p. 142 ff.) turns out to be unspectacular in itself. The topography is described in a low key or else parodied (the town is called Bally, but you must say 'Ballyba when you mean Bally plus its domains and Ballybaba when you mean the domains exclusive of Bally itself', pp. 143–4). Moran relates his adventures and sufferings – even the killing of a stranger who is looking for someone like Molloy, and his long separation from his son – in a tone that ranges from self-alienation to weary resignation (in contrast to Molloy's vivid narrative in Part One).

What comes into focus with growing clarity and emotion is Moran's gradual self-transformation (at one point he is gazing at his own image in the stream, like Narcissus at the pool, p. 156) and his scrupulous self-narration. What he records is, essentially, the story of progressive diminishment. In only three days his physical condition deteriorates spectacularly, and without apparent cause (as always in Beckett): first the pain in his knee incapacitates him; then he starts ageing 'as swiftly as a day-fly', a strange Kafkaesque metamorphosis that feels like 'crumbling, a frenzied collapsing of all I was condemned to be' (p. 159). On the subject of the self, Moran is both eloquent and precise in these final sequences, as when he comments on his own images of degeneration, including his distorted face:

But I confess I attended but absently to these poor figures, in which I suppose my sense of disaster sought to contain itself. And that I did not labour at them more diligently was a further index of the great changes I had suffered and of my growing resignation of being dispossessed of self.

(p. 160)

Such an explicit confession underlines what has been the main thrust of Moran's otherwise increasingly empty voyage of discovery – towards dispossession of self (a key link with the other two novels in the trilogy). We assume that here we are witnessing a process of diminishment that parallels Molloy's narrative. And, true to that pattern, the searcher virtually collapses before any trace of his goal (his 'prey') can be found. The quest for Molloy fades out as the quest for the mother had done. Moran's homecoming – on Gaber's abruptly and mindlessly delivered order: 'Moran, Jacques, home, instanter' (p. 175) – can then be seen as 'fulfilment' through disintegration. For not only is Moran almost destroyed by the long winter journey back, without help and provisions, but he finds his home deserted – a dead place, with the hens, the bees, and all created things, dead.

Moran responds to these sights with ambiguous death-in-life/life-in-death impulses: he thinks he may 'make an end', but also thinks that perhaps he will meet Molloy. He is recognised by one of the neighbours (one of the Elsner sisters) and by the surviving birds of the air. That dual pattern is again mythic, presenting an emotionally charged landscape, with universal symbols like the partial recovery of the waste garden. It is appropriate that when the end is almost reached, Moran should hear a voice telling him to write a report – a fiction, a lying truth. The end of his narrative simply draws attention to the beginning – the circular structure and the fictionality of all that we have been told.

Narrative, voice and writing

First person narrative is almost as old as the novel itself and it has been used by a large number of novelists, including Dickens and Proust, to mime an autobiographical tone. Beckett has transformed this convention into an unmistakable new voice: the narrator/narrated (a term he once used in a letter). This embraces the unstable and exploratory self-revelations of the teller – beyond and across the 'story' – in the process of telling, or ill-telling, that story. If the 'I'-narrator's ability to narrate is necessarily limited (in contrast to the omniscient narrator) by what he knows directly, such a limitation is intensified by Beckett into something like a crippling defect which turns into a gift. For not only is the narrator frequently ignorant about his 'material' (the past), but he keeps losing control over his 'writing' here and now – despite a paradoxically high level of verbal control and literary articulateness. From the narrator's handicap stems much of the difficulty as well as the humour (the parody and the metafiction) in the trilogy. (See also chapter 7 above).

So a novel like *Molloy*, approximately miming autobiography, cannot be kept stable, for the 'material' (memories of a past self) and the 'writing' (an often disturbed present consciousness) keep intersecting or merging in a fluid way. And the 'writing' refuses to be smoothed out or edited into complete fictional coherence. On the contrary, it shows up its own interruptions, gaps, overlaps and contradictions, above all the narrator's conflicts and indecisions – often the nodal point of pain. (Among many examples, see Moran's difficult siesta meditation, briefly discussed above.)

Such an approach dispenses with most of the reassuring constants of the traditional novel: stable myth, character, setting, events and objects, together with an underlying belief that the fictional world 'corresponds' to the external world we know, and that the causes and sequences of the plotted story 'follow'. Instead, a series of uncertainties are introduced into the narrative which can be seen most sharply in three aspects of *Molloy*: the overlapping two-part narration; the presence of the self-conscious and style-conscious writer in the texture of writing; and the built-in randomness in all the major aspects of story-telling.

We may start with the broadest feature: the overlap of Molloy and Moran. On the mythic level, and taking Moran's solitary vision as our guide, we have already seen how Moran, in his at first banal-seeming quest for Molloy, gradually leans into the imaginative world of that 'fabulous being' – until he takes on some of Molloy's weaknesses and is driven through stages of, perhaps salutary, self-diminishment. On the structural level, numerous parallels correspond to this mythic merging of the two narrator-heroes. There is the crucial circumstance that both set out on a quest (though only Moran obeys an order given by some outside power) and both are compelled to write a report on their long and ultimately futile journey. In the course of that journey, Molloy enters a forest and Moran stays on the edge of a forest (the Dante image); both hear a gong; both meet two strangers, make use of a bicycle while they are still tolerably fit, and both use a crutch (Moran only after his return); both have strange encounters with strangers – Molloy assaults a charcoal-burner and Moran murders someone who resembles him. Further, they share some physical and other features: their testicles hang low; they tend to be obsessed by numerical order (Molloy's sucking stones, Moran's shirt), and each wears a hat tied by a string that breaks. They might well be considered split-off aspects of one personality – a kind of Jekyll and Hyde pair, with hints and groping cross-references taking the place of the traditional 'spelling out' of the features of doubling.

On the level of narrating/writing we do have two distinct voices, never more marked than in the opening of Moran's report (so different from Molloy's winding monologue, as we have seen): the complacent voice of the self-respecting, that is, the self-suppressing, bourgeois. Their styles of narration remain distinct for major sections of the two-part novel, though Moran eventually acquires even some of Molloy's verbal richness – and his struggles with the language – in certain key passages which we have quoted. In short, they can hardly be 'the same' writer, though they have a kinship – as if they were aspects of one writer, or partnered writers separated by a great space that is diminishing as Moran's quest unfolds. But here, too, there remain considerable uncertainties, for the initial sharp opposition of Moran and Molloy – as rational/irrational, controlled/unconsciously guided – is deliberately erased as the two writers approximate each other. There is a pattern, but it will not be reduced to a scheme.

Let us now consider the self- and style-conscious narrator. It might be tempting to simplify the uncertainties in the overlapping narratorial voices by saying, 'well, of course, Beckett as author is behind both these voices, playing variations, doubling up'. The temptation is strengthened by the sudden eruption of a kind of 'voice-over' connecting several characters across the range of Beckett's pre-trilogy fiction:

Oh the stories I could tell you if I were easy. What a rabble in my head, what a gallery of moribunds. Murphy, Watt, Yerk, Mercier, and all the others. I would never have believed that – yes I believe it willingly.

(p. 147)

This looks like a version of the direct authorial comment, once practised by English novelists from Fielding to Thackeray. It is a device where the narrator's self-parody draws attention to the assumed author of this novel and the *other* novels for good measure: attention, this is my book, my fiction – signed S.B. (an effect to be repeated in the other two novels of the trilogy). The device interrupts and distances the reader, in a way similar to the direct references to being in the theatre in Beckett's early plays (Beckett's version of the Brechtian 'alienation effect'). At the same time, we may accept that there is a constant and irrepressible autobiographical or confessional urge behind almost all of Beckett's work (see Introduction p. 3), but this urge is always thoroughly fictionalised, in the present instance in the figure of the writer wrestling with the burden of all those unique but remarkably similar incarnations – narrator-heroes.

As writer–narrators Molloy and Moran share various formal and stylistic obsessions. Both produce cyclic stories, where the end returns us to the beginning. (Moran's ironic conclusion advertises fiction as 'lies', unstable and unreliable narration: 'It is midnight.' / 'It was not midnight.') This may provide a key to the ceaseless reflexive pointing to fiction-making throughout the novel(s): the emphatic presence of the troubled writer. The self-mirroring narrator intervenes and so to speak grimaces – like a deliberately ill-equipped guide to his own story-telling – as he moves into the foreground.

Once this is seen, a large number of pieces fall into place in the mosaic of writing about writing, above all the voice of the reluctant, the weary or the failing writer – who sees the futility of each sentence even as he is shaping it – anticipating defeat before the start. The tone is ambivalent, triumphantly despairing:

you would do better, at least no worse, to obliterate texts than to blacken margins, to fill in the holes of words till all is blank and flat and the whole ghastly business looks like what it is, senseless, speechless, issueless misery.

(Molloy's report, pp. 13–14)

This can be compared to Moran, who has an almost paranoid sense of obligation towards his task-masters, seeing the act of writing as a labour of Sisyphus (alluding to the myth of the incessantly re-punished stone-roller, which Camus used as the representative metaphor for modern man's sense of absurdity in a famous essay published in 1941):

But I write [these lines] all the same, and with a firm hand weaving inexorably back and forth and devouring my page with the indifference of a shuttle . . .

And it would not surprise me if I deviated, in the pages to follow, from the true and exact succession of events. But I do not think even Sisyphus is required to scratch himself, or to groan, or to rejoice, as the fashion is now, always at the same appointed places. (pp. 142-3)

In this passage the word 'penance' is also applied to the task of writing; elsewhere it is called a 'pensum' (the old word for a school task, still used to denote the compulsory syllabus at Nordic universities). The great burden of writing is partly the re-telling of the past ('that must again be unknown to me') in a proper order, when perhaps there cannot be a proper order. A fundamental doubt on this score necessarily affects the writing, whenever it touches on time and place, on sequence, on identity, names and naming – all the supposed fixed points of the traditional art of fiction. All these are drawn into the shifting uncertainties of memory and language. In the end the fixed points of fiction cannot be 'pinned down', for the act of writing itself – even the grammar, the shifting tenses – may loosen them like tent-poles in the sand.

We have already seen how each of the central character/narrators – Moran and Molloy – undergo significant transformations, the former in the direction of the latter. If Molloy is a mythical being, he springs from a singularly unstable or composite myth; if Moran is an agent, he is a hybrid from many different kinds of narrative ranging from detective fiction to allegory. Not surprisingly, the uncertainty pervades all the characters or, more properly, the figures that cross the landscape of the journey. The remarkable episode of A and C, immediately following the prologue (pp. 8-15), gains some of its impact from the way Molloy can express a longing to meet one of them, as if wishing to be reunited with a separated father, without 'having a clue' about the identity of the passer-by, and without being able to experience more than the semblance of contact with him. He is not even sure whether A and C are altogether distinct from himself: 'People pass too, hard to distinguish from yourself. That is discouraging. So I saw A and C going slowly towards each other, unconscious of what they were doing.' And, after a sustained meditation on the appearance of one of these strangers – probably C – Molloy repeats his doubts about A and C being altogether distinct from each other:

And perhaps it was A one day at one place, then C another at another, then a third the rock and I, and so on for the other components, the cows, the sky, the sea, the mountains. I can't believe it. No, I will not lie, I can easily conceive it. No matter, no matter, let us go on, as if all arose from the same weariness, on and on, heaping up and up, until there is no room, no light, for any more. (p. 15)

'Perhaps' is the keyword here, perhaps. For the narrator to confess uncertainty about such major elements in the narrative – the
identity of a character, the timing and sequence of events – ends
by something very near to total scepticism regarding the world as
it is perceived, and as it is written about (not 'represented' or
'reflected') in a work of fiction. The uncertainties of experience
and perception are then squared, so to speak, by the uncertainties
of writing.

The grammar of narrative itself seems to buckle at certain
points, in this highly articulate prose, as when the narrator suddenly announces: 'This should all be re-written in the pluperfect.'
(p. 17) or 'What I assert, deny, question, in the present, I still can.
But mostly I shall use the various tenses of the past. For mostly
I do not know, it is perhaps no longer so, it is too soon to know,
I simply do not know, perhaps shall never know' (p. 113). The
tenses inevitably prove inadequate when the time of the narrative
cannot be pinned down by the 'ignorant' narrator.

I say that now, *but after all what do I know now of then* now when the icy
words hail down upon me, the icy meanings, and the world dies too, foul-
ly named. *All I know is what the words know*, and the dead things, and that
makes a handsome little sum, with a beginning, a middle and an end as
in the well-built phrase and the long sonata of the dead.

(p. 33, emphasis added)

Uncertainty concerning time, place and identity extends, not
surprisingly, to object, whether seen, contemplated or acquired by
the narrator. Thus Molloy reports having stolen from Lousse a
silver object – probably a knife rest – in a language that singles
it out, gives it significance: '[it] haunts me still'; 'it consisted of
two crosses joined, at their points of intersection, by a bar'; 'for
a certain time I think it inspired me with a kind of veneration' (pp.
67–8). But in the actual narration, the accumulation of 'insigni-
ficant' detail concerning the two identical V shapes mocks and
undermines the signifying vocabulary. The silver object is then
freed from any fixed value, personal or cultural (a 'keepsake', a
Christian symbol) or even material (to be exchanged for food
when hungry). Rather like Molloy's famous sucking stones (pp.
72–9) – an arbitrary permutational game – the silver object is
then open to any number of interpretations: 'I could therefore
puzzle over it *endlessly* without the least risk' (p. 68, emphasis
added. This sentence precedes the passage on 'beyond knowing
anything' quoted on p. 113).

123

When the narrative itself undermines any sign towards a possible fixed interpretation, it presents an appearance of randomness at every level. We can see how conscious and controlled that random effect is from sudden mock-philosophical statements: 'And when it comes to neglecting fundamentals, I think I have nothing to learn, and indeed I confuse them with accidentals' (p. 85). The aim is to end the old hierarchy of narration which subordinates 'accidentals' to 'fundamentals' and has a fixed place for all significant elements: the cross-like object would then be a Christian symbol, the house of Lousse the place of enchantment we know from romance, and Molloy a well-defined mythic or allegorical hero. Instead, a kind of principle of uncertainty enters the dual narrative of *Molloy* – 'no symbols where none intended', in the words of the final sentence of *Watt* (1953). The openness of writing invites an openness of reader response, in a new type of fiction that is to be further explored, fundamentally varied and intensified in the other two volumes of the trilogy.

9

Malone Dies

For a dying man to write his memoirs seems, at first sight, a simple extension of a certain kind of literary memoir in which – from Dostoevsky's *Notes from Underground* (1864) to Saul Bellow's *Dangling Man* (1944) – the narrator gives an account of himself in an extreme state of isolation, talking to himself on the brink of the void. At the same time, the memoir will also be seen as an extension of *Molloy*, taking the quest of that novel towards a physical and metaphoric conclusion. There is an affinity between the worlds of the two novels, over and above the specific signs that link Malone to Molloy: the large, hairy head, the hat with the string, while Macmann's possessions include a silver knife-rest – the object Molloy stole from Lousse. It is possible to visualise Malone as a Molloy-like figure diminished by extreme age (and he has been so presented in a dramatised version by the Irish actor Barry McGovern). Nevertheless, the scope and structure of this novel are quite different, beginning with its fundamental elimination of movement in space – of the epic voyage – and the placing of the 'hero' in complete confinement. (All we know is that he is in a room, in an ordinary house that sometimes sounds like an asylum.) Molloy as narrator is also confined and immobile, but his mobile memories still create the illusion of tramp-like wandering across a spacious mythic landscape. By contrast, Malone is totally circumscribed by his cell-sized room; and his minimal capacity for movement (for example, getting hold of the dish and the chamber-pot with his stick), offers a grotesque mockery of the human body's vaunted athletic prowess. The immobility is sustained (as in plays like *Krapp's Last Tape* and *Happy Days*), condemning a trapped person to unending soliloquising.

While this kind of immobility (stasis) is now indelibly associated with the 'Beckett world' as a primary metaphor, it was an innovation for *Malone Dies* – a new departure, abandoning further remnants of external narrative, picaresque detail, character, placing and naming. Those aspects of traditional fiction still surface in Malone's attempts at story-telling, as an escape from his dying consciousness into 'another', a fictional creature. That level is at least as significant as our present starting point – the consciously dying self.

The final diminishment of the self

Dying is here a prolonged process of reflective waiting ('the waiting that knows itself in vain', p. 84), and also a play or a game (p. 6). (Waiting and playing foreshadow the structural themes, respectively, of *Waiting for Godot*, written immediately after *Malone Dies*, and of *Endgame*.) Some of the vigorous humour – 'gallows' humour – of the early plays also accompanies this adventure of slow dying. For a dying man, Malone begins with a remarkably robust prologue: 'For the year is still young, a thousand little signs tell me so. Perhaps I am wrong, perhaps I shall survive St John the Baptist's Day and even the Fourteenth of July festival of freedom.' (This reference to French public holidays is typical for a work first written in French; on the other hand, the Malone world, the setting, has an Irish scenery, especially in the concluding sections.) The writer of those pre-death memoirs is often to address us with a garrulous energy, like Shakespeare's dying John of Gaunt. The idea of death concentrates his mind. Here there is no senility, in the commonly understood sense, but rather a clear-headed stock-taking, coupled with a certain exhilaration over actual and anticipated symptoms of decay: worse is better, less is more . . . He is looking forward, among other things, to diminished consciousness of *self* (a pious hope which the reader justifiably expects to be ironic, since such a writer cannot write a sentence without referring back to the self):

I shall pay less heed to myself, I shall be neither hot nor cold any more, I shall be tepid, I shall die tepid, without enthusiasm. I shall not watch myself die, that would spoil everything. (p. 8)

Malone's preparation for death is ironically exemplary, in one respect worthy of a Victorian patrician preparing to make his will. His attitude towards his minimal belongings, destitute and without children or any relation as he is, has an air of pedantic possessiveness. He appears to cling to what he wishes to discard, and numerous sections of his narrative can be seen as notes towards the inventory he promises himself. Indeed, writing about his present state is itself a kind of inventory – of left-over limbs and faculties. It is often nearer to an exhibition than to a penance. The body's decrepitude is related with circumstantial relish in several passages: his feebleness and immobility ('Sometimes I miss not being able to crawl around any more. But I am not much given to nostalgia', p. 14); the dimming of his senses, the gradual dying of the light and of sounds; and the decay of his genitals. (Malone presents his own impotence – as later the grotesque

126

love-making of Macmann and Moll – with an irony more savage than in Swift, mock-diagnostic precision followed by mock-resignation: 'I do not expect to see my sex again, with my naked eye, not that I wish to, we've stared at each other long enough, in the eye, but it gives you some idea', p. 63.)

By contrast, the attempts to speak of inner states – of the suffering soul – are tentative, groping, yet they reach a deeper level of self-awareness and negative mysticism than did Molloy's search for self. For Malone the fundamental question of dying is to be the question of whether a true or timeless self can be reached on the threshold of death. Beyond suffering and 'the stupid flesh' ('I shall not speak of my sufferings. Cowering deep down among them I feel nothing. It is there I die, unbeknown to my stupid flesh' pp. 14–15), Malone is concerned with his 'soul', a word used ambivalently, as essence (a non-material, non-mortal self), and as nothingness (the vacancy of non-being). The ambivalence forms part of Beckett's profound agnosticism. 'And in the skull is it a vacuum? I ask' is the question that precedes this litany:

as it were the soul that must be veiled, that soul denied in vain, vigilant, anxious, turning in its cage as in a lantern, in the night without haven or craft or matter or understanding. Ah yes, I have my little pastimes and they . . .   (p. 50)

This soul-searching deepens, and reaches a desperate intensity in the next section (pp. 50–4), interwoven with the little comedy of Malone looking for his lost pencil and his mislaid exercise book. In a series of overlapping images, the narrator's sense of being is suspended between dying and birth, between 'the blessedness of absence' (left behind by something 'unutterable like the crumbling away of two little heaps of finest sand, or dust, or ashes, of unequal size but diminishing together' p. 51) and a freakish and problematic pre-natal or foetal stage:

Yes, an old foetus, that's what I am now, hoar and impotent, mother is done for, I've rotted her, she'll drop me with the help of gangrene, perhaps papa is at the party too, I'll land head-foremost mewling in the charnel-house, not that I'll mewl, not worth it.   (p. 54)

This violent image of birth-into-death (contrast the more lyrical image in Vladimir's speech in *Waiting for Godot* (pp. 90–1): 'Astride of a grave and a difficult birth . . . the grave-digger puts on the forceps') is immediately followed by an outright negation: 'No, the answer is no, I shall never get born and therefore never get dead, and a good job too.' Such a categorical negation would

rule out a religious or Romantic 'dying-into-life' or re-birth interpretation of Malone's speculations on death. Beyond that, Malone
appears to despair of ever being able to reach his 'I' – his essential or true self – even on the threshold of dying. And, in the logic
of paradox (recalling the paradoxes of the mystics or of Donne and
Metaphysical poetry) what cannot be born, cannot die. The feeling of not having a self is here pushed to an extreme point where
the notion of 'I shall never get born . . . dead' is pitted against
the centre of our I-centred identity. That sense of identity has
been dominant and almost universal in Western culture: from the
spiritual/Pauline 'by the grace of God I am what I am' – or else
the plain 'I am I' – to the long-pondered rational/Cartesian affirmation 'I think therefore I am.' To all these the Malone memoir
says: 'No'. (Malone's negation is worked out further in *The
Unnamable* and in the short play *Not I*, whose title epitomises the
pain of this condition.) Towards the end of Malone's narrative,
another birth-into-death image – the barely viable foetus and its
breech delivery – is introduced in a grotesque form:

I am being given, if I may venture the expression, birth to into death
[*sic*], such is my impression. The feet are clear already, of the great cunt
of existence. Favourable presentation I trust. My head will be the last to
die.   (p. 113)

With such fundamental scepticism concerning his own chances
of essential or ultimate being, it is hardly surprising that Malone
should have doubts about the time and place, the merely outward
and still observable circumstances of his present state. Even
though this present reality is sketched in with enough details to
provide a seemingly 'realistic' story (the room itself, his few
objects, his view from the window; later his visitor, the blow on
his head, and so on), Malone's patient or impatient waiting for
death is located in a no-place. It is not specific, that room in a
nondescript house, in contrast to Macmann's asylum (see below,
pp. 136ff.). It has some of the (unmistakably Beckettian) attributes
of limbo, purgatory or hell, as when he thinks that perhaps he is
'dead already' ('Perhaps I expired in the forest, or even earlier'
(p. 48) – another link with Molloy). Again, in the long meditation on silence and the self, preceding the passage on the soul,
quoted above, p. 127, Malone wonders whether his present world
is not wholly in the mind:

You may say it is all in my head, and indeed sometimes it seems to me I am
in a head and that these eight, no six, these six planes that enclose me are of
solid bone. But thence to conclude the head is mine, no, never.   (p. 50)

It is fitting that such an end-place should have no *light* proper any longer, only variations of a diffused grey light – a 'leaden light that makes no shadow', lighting a place where there is no colour, only a 'kind of grey incandescence' (p. 49).

Time itself is unmeasurable (Malone, unlike Pozzo, makes no mention of any timepiece): it alternately contracts to a tedious present or expands to a timeless vastness. *Malone Dies* is not presented as a memoir of memories (as *Molloy* was) and so what it tells the reader of time past is very restricted. There are some eight statements in all, with only a few references to what may have happened before Malone was brought to this room – he suffers from what sounds like partial amnesia. But the odd childhood memory may suddenly surface – through a chance association, breaking the present narration – like the recall of 'the hearing of my boyhood' (the sound of 'the leaves, the boughs, the groaning trunks, even the grasses', p. 34), or first seeing an aeroplane, ('I was present at one of the first loopings of the loop, so help me God' – when reporting on his visitor, p. 97). Otherwise time is essentially centred on time present, as in most of the plays. The future-oriented waiting for death (from the opening 'ungrammatical' future tense of the memoir: 'I shall soon be quite dead at last despite of all'), does, nevertheless, create a counter-present. That waiting brings its own suspense, against the mere stagnation (stasis) of an everlasting present moment. There is no journal-like chronology, only an occasional remark on the uncertain passing of the seasons. Although there is a kind of sequence – Malone's diminishing physical and psychic control – the sense of time is almost suspended throughout Malone's reflections. What he says in a section of a Macmann story also applies to his own apprehension of events in time:

Little by little the haze formed again, and the sense of absence, and the captive things began to murmur again, each one to itself, and it was as if nothing had ever happened or would ever happen again.   (p. 109)

This pattern of 'nothing happening' is, again, one that we now take for granted in Beckett's work, but it had to be worked out, as a new and original pattern, in and for *Malone Dies*. Inescapably, an immobilised and decrepit person feels that the whole horizon of experience is shrinking. But how is this extreme passivity to be expressed so as to move forward – as narrative? How is the progressive/regressive inanition of a person made to yield up the depths of certain experiences? How does a mind that submits to an engulfing sense of nothingness find the material, let alone the energy, for a confessional? ('I shall write my memoirs. That's funny, I have made a joke', p. 12.) Malone's inability to recall the past (except in flashes) might be thought to inhibit the driving force of an autobiography. Neither has he brought into his final isolation urgent 'problems', tasks or even perceptions; he is not quite the challenging thinker; still less is he like a prisoner in a death-cell obsessed by a utopian future. He is a diminished person. His obsessions turn out to be a few curious variations on what it is like to be deprived – grain by grain – of a sense of selfhood. But, aided by an exercise book and a diminishing pencil, he fills the time of dying with the act of writing – his consuming activity, his compulsive task. And gradually the act of writing becomes the main interest of the novel.

Before we turn to writing as Malone's main resource, it is worth recalling the extent of his passivity. The opening sections have mapped out the tiny territory of his room (bed, cupboard, cherished objects) leaving only one outlet from totally immured vision – the window. Through that window he can see two other windows and so into the room of the house opposite: a kind of cinema-screen that promises to show something else than self-projection. Acts of gazing into a window beyond his window (like a voyeur) becomes Malone's link or 'umbilicus' (p. 52) with the external world, his most other-directed activity (apart from the characters in his stories before they begin to merge into himself). Early on (when he interrupts the Sapo story, pp. 19–20), Malone watches a woman for an instant 'coming and going' behind the window where the light has just been turned on. Later, in the long soliloquy that interrupts the Macmann story (pp. 67ff.), Malone sees in the window, behind the curtain, two figures who 'cleave so fast together that they seem a single body'. He follows up this observation with mock-learned speculations, until he stumbles on the remarkable hypothesis that he has been witnessing an amorous embrace. Through that window fragments of nature may also be glimpsed, for example the night sky (like a romantic landscape by Kaspar David Friedrich, a typical Beckett association), until 'words and images run riot in my head, pursuing, flying, clashing, merging, endlessly' (p. 26). Like a poet who is moved, but whose shaping imagination has not yet found or disciplined a proper object, Malone's whirling mind multiplies the strands in his soliloquy. Out of his state of impotence, and a minimal 'spray of phenomena', the writer's words multiply. The energy of that process may at times suggest a young man's internal monologue – with shades of Joyce's Stephen – rather than an old man's dying thoughts. But then Beckett is not concerned with 'representing' old age, but with finding a voice that can enact its own decay.

Malone's gradual diminishment accelerates in the final sequences of the novel – a process presented with great economy. The old woman no longer comes to bring him food or empty his pots; instead he has a visit from a menacing stranger whom he first takes to be the undertaker's man calling prematurely. Malone then feels a 'violent blow on the head' and he thinks that he has been hit by the stranger, but neither the action nor its possible motive is at any point clarified. The episode has a hallucinatory character and it tallies with Malone's deteriorating condition, his failing voice, his migraine, his growing difficulty in writing, as death approaches. The blow on his head could be a projection of an inner pain, a fit or a stroke – the reader cannot decide, and such an interpretation would not change the overall effect of a death agony. The irruption of violence in Malone's final phase soon finds an analogue in the hideous violence of Lemuel, the new 'nurse' who kills those under his charge with a hatchet – in the Macmann story (see below, pp. 136–7). The gradual convergence of the memoir and the story told, and the growing uncertainty – the blurring of outlines – is itself a symptom of fading consciousness. As if through sympathetic magic, Malone's left-over possessions have been diminishing in synchrony with his body–mind: the stick slips from his grasp at one point; the exercise book has to be hidden from the visitor; the pencil is getting shorter and shorter. And in the memorable ending (quoted on p. 105 above) the story-in-progress, the pencil, and the story-teller's consciousness – his life, we are made to feel – diminish and fade out inseparably.

Narration as self-reflection and failure

Malone is probably the first fictional 'hero' who both narrates himself and, in the gaps of his memoir (first person, present tense), composes fragments of fiction (incomplete, third-person, past tense stories concerning Sapo, and then Macmann). Both the memoir and the stories are subject to a recurrent and free-ranging commentary around and beyond these core-texts: the meta-memoir is concerned mostly with sessions of thought on the self, and the meta-stories mostly with questions of writing. These four levels of text are subtly – and far from regularly – intercalated and tend to overlap. However, the main sections are marked by clear gaps in some editions (unfortunately not in the Calder edition). There are also clear internal markers, usually in the words that introduce a section, to indicate a shift of focus. For example, in the following sequence:

(a) I fear I must have fallen asleep again (the memoir).
(b) I have just written, I fear I must have fallen, etc. (meta-memoir, talking about problems of self, but also about the pencil and the exercise book and character creation – see below).
(c) The summer holidays [of Sapo] were drawing to a close (story).
(d) What tedium. If I went on to the stone? No it would be the same thing (meta-story, or meditation on the story merging into self-reflection).   (pp. 37–44)

The text overall has a clarity and a lightness which many readers will find easier to follow than the supposedly continuous narrative of *Molloy* Part One. All the attempts at story-telling are soon revealed to be aids to the narrator's search for the elusive true self – while his body–mind is dying. At the same time, it is also an escape from the self (the recurrent function of fictionalising in Beckett). Each story he tells is an attempt 'to depart from myself' into 'another': a NOT I. But, at a certain point, each new tale coils back like a spring to its teller – the teller's condition, consciousness and language. The teller can't step over his shadow.

Looking beyond this particular novel, we become aware of a recurrent feature of Beckett's fiction: the soliloquising narrator finds it increasingly difficult, if not impossible, to create a third-person story with 'other' characters who might speak from the centre of a wholly different consciousness. We are a long way here from what Keats admired in Shakespeare: an equal delight in wholly different creations, an Iago and a Desdemona, through 'negative capability', or what the Russian critic Bakhtin calls the dialogic consciousness, in the novels of Dostoevsky. Instead, Beckett's creative energy goes into the realisation of ever-new variants for an inescapably inward and monologic universe of fiction (see also pp. 105–6 above).

At the simplest level, Malone's story-telling urge is a time-killing device. Static time seems infinite, and infinitely oppressive, even when brief and limited in duration. The shrinking consciousness of the dying man nails every second to his present condition. So the stories provide an object beyond the personal emptiness, a refuge from the circling obsessions of a depleted mind. Chronic boredom, we know from autobiographies, has driven a certain type of writer to writing, and a political prisoner in solitary confinement has owed her sane survival to the daily recall of characters from the novels of Dickens. In *Malone Dies* such a strategy of survival is given an ironic twist, as Malone does not *want* to survive but to die. He does not stand in awe of death – like Christian in the Valley of the Shadow of Death – nor does he prepare himself for dying 'well', as in certain types of religious exercise, for example in Jeremy Taylor's *The Rule and Exercises of Holy Dying* (1651). He does not set himself a purpose, though we may interpret the complexities of trying to find the (essential) self as just such a purpose.

More complex is Malone's desire – as author or fictionaliser – to create 'another'. It is an irrational urge that has some Romantic undertones, though it is more a blind, obsessive self-imposed task to write and go on *writing*. (Malone does not obey an 'order' as Molloy and Moran do.) Then failure becomes the paradoxical goal:

After the fiasco, the solace, the repose, I began again, to try to live, cause to live, by another, in myself, in another [. . .] But little by little with a different aim, no longer in order to succeed, but in order to fail.

(p. 23)

These ambivalent attitudes ('try to live, cause to live' versus aiming at failure) are present everywhere in Malone's stories and meta-stories. Thus in another authorial commentary (p. 37), a version of the sublime-sounding project – 'to live, and cause to live, at last, to play at last and die alive' – is cancelled out by a confession of defeat: 'the plan I had formed was going the way of all my other plans' (p. 37). This is written in the context of growing narratorial fatigue: 'I do not depart from myself now with the same avidity as a week ago for example.' Various kinds of pedantic emendations of his text open, and a stream of spirited reflections on his exercise book and pencil close this section. The familiar urge to write about anything rather than 'the matter in hand' then creeps into the story of the Saposcats, with its abrupt closures, repetitions and comic editorial interruptions: 'What tedium' (p. 15, cf. pp. 17, 19).

These fluctuations, between something very like creative joy and a contrary weariness, are written into the texture of the stories. On the one hand, each story in succession – the Saposcats with the Lamberts, Macmann with Lemuel and the fatal excursion – has a vigour, a precision and an unusual degree of 'realistic' detail, at least on the local level. At the same time, each story peters out at a certain point, getting merged with, or submerged under, other narratives: Sapo the youth is transformed into the ancient Macmann, who in turn begins to resemble the figure of Malone. In this way we get a sense of inescapable instability – in the narrator's mind, and, inseparably from it, in the flow of words, in the act of writing itself.

Thus the novel parody (so robust in *Murphy* and in the opening sequences of both parts of *Molloy*) becomes more fragile and self-destructive in *Malone Dies* (but still at several removes from the Unnamable's self-dissolution). Here the writing itself is being seen through. The writer feels that he cannot win in the game of writing. Whatever his initial success in a particular story, the story recoils from him or he from the story. The character imagined, 'the other', may begin to resemble the narrator too closely, and thus provoke creative dissatisfaction:

What tedium. And I call that playing. I wonder if I am not talking yet again about myself. Shall I be incapable, to the end, of lying on any other subject? (p. 17)

Conversely, the character imagined may seem too remote from the narrator's own 'self-image', in which case he/she becomes ripe for being disowned – like Sapo the young adult, as he grows more and more into a dullish character, and like the inferior character suggested by one of Malone's authorial ironies: 'My concern is not with me, but with another, far beneath me and whom I try to envy, of whose crass adventures I can now tell, at last, I don't know how' (p. 24).

In sum, Malone's design – to tell himself stories which have little or nothing to do with his own condition – fails. Fragments of autobiography are perceptible between the lines, usually in the shape of curious parallels. It is a subtle pattern, at first obscured by the vigorously externalised story sections. For example, the story of Sapo (homo sapiens, cf. Man-alone, Mac-Man/n) begins as a savoury piece full of 'local colour': the poor boy struggling for an education. And the narrator's delight in the act of narration – despite his protestations of 'tedium' – is constantly fed into the

134

text. ('A few words about the boy. This cannot be avoided' . . .
'He attended his classes with his mind elsewhere. He liked sums,
but not the way they were taught.') But soon, by the second page
of the Sapo story, we have this kind of tacit rather than direct
authorial comment: 'It was as though the Saposcats drew the
strength to live from the prospect of their impotence' (p. 16). At
such a point, the Malone style (or the Beckett style), which is also
a dimension, can be seen to deepen and extend the story-within-
the-memoir: the well-etched portrait of a good-natured, dull boy
begins to show affinities with the narrator's own state. By the
second major section of the Sapo story, the narrator (not content
with a leisurely first-person authorial mumbling) tags on to the
main narrative an intrusive comment, with a shift into first
person:

But Sapo was not expelled, either then or later. I must try and discover,
when I have time to think about it quietly, why Sapo was not expelled
when he so richly deserved to be. For I want as little as possible darkness
in this story.
(p. 18)

By the next paragraph, we have the 'answer': 'I have not been
able to find out why Sapo was not expelled. I shall have to leave
this question open.' This is impertinent – not pertinent – in the
manner of Sterne's parodic narrative. It is the manner of the
omniscient narrator claiming to know little or nothing about his
characters – being omni-impotent as it were. 'Darkness' is
deliberately brought into the story (the stories) being told, to correspond with the deepening darkness of the dying narrator.

Such parallels abound in the story of the Lamberts, which is
connected with the Sapo story by only the thin thread of Sapo's
visit to the Lamberts' house. It is another robust-seeming story,
with a marked realistic bent. (In French it sounds in places like
Balzac, even before one is told that Beckett did have in mind a
realistic Balzac novel, *Louis Lambert*.) Yet the vivid little details of
rural life (the dead mule, the sorting of lentils, etc.) are again shot
through with self-reflecting details – with pauses and brooding
lyrical passages. Their melancholy tone itself points back to the
story-teller's sensibility. For example, in the sustained sequence
beginning 'In the filthy kitchen' (pp. 30–4) Sapo can hear (beyond
the daughter calling the goats and the father cursing his mule) the
silence 'in the heart of the dark, the silence of dust and the things
that would never stir'. Again, in the house of the Lamberts, 'the
face of Sapo was as always grave, or rather expressionless. And

when he halted it was . . . simply because the voice had ceased that told him to go on' (p. 34). In a later section of the story (pp. 40ff.), it is the death of animals that is related with strongly felt compassion (for example, the 'rabbits that die before they are killed, from sheer fright' . . . 'And often you strike a corpse without knowing it', (p. 43), while in the section on Mrs Lambert her daily round of toil is presented with a melancholy inwardness ('From the well of this unending weariness her sigh went up unendingly, for day when it was night, for night when it was day . . .' in a cadenced, nine-line sentence, p. 45). The character's state of mind, the world of phenomena observed, and the style which mediates all that, jointly permeate the story with the narrator's consciousness and language. The tragic sense, and the weariness, concerning 'the way things are', gradually merges into the narratorial dissatisfaction with the inadequacy of the story. The narrator's own pathos and conscious self-depletion is inscribed in his otherwise robust short stories. And the gratuitous narratorial commentary – the meta-story – tells us what the story itself shows: how the writing tires of itself, caught up in its own subjects and words, in diminishing circles.

The Macmann story is, from the start, presented from a point of view several moves nearer to the narrator's condition. Macmann's arrival and treatment in the asylum deliberately suggests Malone's situation in a more extreme version. Further, Macmann has a distinct 'family likeness' to other trilogy characters, notably to Molloy (as already suggested) through his advanced age, his decrepitude, and through some of his possessions – his greatcoat, hat, and silver knife-rest. And on the meta-narratorial level, Malone-as-narrator finally abandons all the remaining constraits of 'objective' narration as he presents Macmann. The authorial intrusions now achieve quite a joyous sense of freedom, which nevertheless implies an enslavement to fiction and writing: 'I have taken a long time to find him again, but I have found him. How did I know it was him, I don't know.' All this self-parody and more before the new-found character is even named, or rather re-named:

For Sapo, no, I can't call him that any more and I even wonder how I was able to stomach such a name till now. So then for, let me see, for Macmann, that's not much better but there is little time to lose, for Macmann might be stark staring naked . . .   (pp. 57–8)

The narratorial hilarity is kept up and developed by recalling that

'Macmanns are legion in the island' (p. 88), so that there might be legitimate doubts concerning this Macmann's continued identity. The adventures of Macmann, if we may call them that, are cut across by forceful comic parody throughout.

First, the superb sequence on Macmann in the rain (pp. 67–75) manages to combine a sense of purgatorial punishment ('and without knowing exactly what his sin was he felt full well that living was not a sufficient atonement for it or that this atonement was itself a sin') with a dramatic pre-Godot action in non-action ('the waiting that knows itself in vain') embodied in his minimal movements on the rain-drenched plain. The climax of Macmann rolling 'along the arc of a gigantic circle probably', in the direction of an assumed dry spot on the plain, is arguably among the best parodic versions of the futile labours of Sisyphus. Macmann's rolling to-and-fro may also be seen as paralleling Malone's tossings and turnings in the bed – the death-bed – without any explicit meta-narratorial analogy. Later, the Macmann and Moll episode – with the savage satire on the grotesque remnants of sexual love – again highlights 'bodily decrepitude' without affirming (as Yeats affirmed) its wisdom. On the contrary, these sketches affirm nothing beyond those diminished body–minds, as they still cling to gestures called love (Macmann's love-letters). In the final phase, the story and the story-teller converge still further: the decline of Macmann corresponds to the final decline of Malone; and Malone's violent killing off of his characters corresponds, we assume, to his violent death-struggle. On one level, these interlinked catastrophes are like the work of a suddenly impatient author who needs a quick end – so his characters must be killed off in a melodramatic carnage for a grand finale. First it is Moll's turn: 'Moll. I am going to kill her' (p. 93). Then Lemuel is created to become the author's obedient executioner in a guignol-like massacre in the midst of Lady Pedal's ironically genteel excursion. Into this deliberately broad parody of a plotted 'ending' are woven, in a concluding fiction, Malone's final lyrical reflections on imminent death: (a) the significant confession: 'All is pretext, Sapo and the birds, Moll the peasants . . . pretext for not coming to the point, the abandoning, the raising of the arms and going down' (p. 106); (b) the extinction of selfhood: 'I shall say I no more' (p. 113); (c) the final fading out of his memoir (quoted earlier), miming both the agony and the slow victory of death 'at last in spite of all'.

The self-conscious narrator becomes, we may conclude from the above reading, increasingly intrusive, despite his self-diminishment, as the novel runs its course. The presence of the writer as a reluctant and ignorant yet compulsively inventive producer of words – a story, then stories within the story and meta-stories around them, and so almost *ad infinitum* – has been deliberately brought into the foreground. In this way *Malone Dies* exhibits its own process of construction while, at significantly placed points, it defeats or de-constructs itself as a novel. Arguably, it is the clearest and best example of such a novel. Malone-as-narrator is the controlling voice at all the levels of narration, but his own 'authorial authority' is itself undermined at times. One of the most striking examples of such a radical device is Malone suddenly stepping out of the role of self-narrating narrator and seeing himself, in effect, as the creator of other characters in other Beckett fictions:

But let us leave these morbid matters and get on with that of my demise, in two or three days if I remember rightly. Then it will be all over with the Murphys, Merciers, Molloys, Morans, and Malones, unless it goes on beyond the grave. (pp. 64–5)

Who is speaking here? Beckett himself as autobiographical commentator? Not quite, for there is still fictionalising. Nor does it sound quite like the intrusive novelist of one tradition of the English novel that existed between Fielding and Dickens. Rather, it is a hybrid voice with a new and distinct kind of utterance. It is the voice of a super-narrator, for whom 'all is pretext' (all characters, all fictions) in the intensified search for the untraced core of the dying self. And that voice is to go on, without a name.

10

The Unnamable

The third novel of the trilogy is a radical innovation, in several
ways an extreme transformation of the elements of Beckett's
writing known to us from the previous two novels. What is left of
fictional character is finally reduced to a disembodied *voice*,
indefinite and indefinable in terms of ordinary human identity,
deprived of specific time, place, function and purpose. In so far
as this voice has a quest – wavering, painful and unsustainable
– it is to find an answer to the questions of its own being, on the
edge of non-being, among shadowy presences in a kind of
limbo. And in so far as it has an aim it is to reach a final silence
through its own excess of speaking: that incessant, compulsive
written soliloquy that makes up the winding text of *The Unnamable*.
If Malone was still driven by a story-telling urge, both to escape
from himself and to make discoveries about the true but dying self,
the Unnamable gets tired of stories almost as soon as he starts one,
and can only summon enough energy to make concrete one out
of four attempted stories – that of Mahood, the torso in the jar.
The other stories, the story of Worm especially, get stunted and
blurred at their inception, barely distinguishable from the 'I'
(unsure of its 'I') that is trying to tell its own non-story. Endless
variations on that uncertain quest, in nervous, rapidly changing
prose rhythms, give the text a force otherwise lacking in situation
and episode.

'Malone is there. Of his mortal liveliness little trace remains',
states the narrator early in the preamble of the novel (p. 8). The
absence of Malone's 'mortal liveliness' may be noted on first
reading *The Unnamable*. And it will soon be realised that the further
diminishment of the narrator/narrated – and of the writing itself:
in terms of story, image, concreteness – 'imitates' the further
diminishment of the mind, virtually disembodied in this furthest
stage of self-exploration.

Malone is still present – in the orbit of the narrator's imagination – repeatedly invoked in the preamble as a generative figure
and seemingly drawn into the narrator's struggle with words
towards a new kind of writing. Indeed, one of the best ways of

entering the rarefied world of *The Unnamable* is to reflect on certain statements in the concluding sections of *Malone Dies*, especially the narrator's ironically plangent tone in looking forward to his own demise: 'Then it will be over with the Murphys, Merciers, Molloys, Morans, and Malones, unless it goes on beyond the grave' (see p. 138 above). Yes, it does go on, from the point of view of the writer writing: the compulsions of the speaking voice, of the word-spinning consciousness, go on – taking the narrator's voice into a limbo-like space, often reminiscent of Dante's inferno. At the same time, the narrator of *The Unnamable* seems to be speaking – like Malone in the passage just quoted – as a kind of super-narrator who stands outside his proper text, and to whom characters and stories are only a pretext for getting on with the desperate search for the lost core of the self. But the Unnamable can also be seen as the opposite of Malone in his narratorial stance: while the latter announces a despairing hope – 'I shall say I no more' – the new narrator will not rest until he can say 'I' in such a way that it convinces the self of its proper being, beyond the fictional personae and the merely casual, contingent 'I' voices. The finding of that essential 'I'-voice would seem to be a precondition for coming to rest, for reaching the ultimate silence constantly talked about.

These new obsessions in the search for the self are set out, in the manner of a philosophical essay, cross-stitched with rhetorical figures, in the seventeen paragraphs of the preamble (pp. 7–20). The preamble illuminates the whole novel and must be given close reading. The urgent opening questions – 'Where now? Who now? When now? – are at once ironically counterpointed by what looks like a statement – 'Unquestioning. I, say I' – but which is in turn undermined within ten lines: 'I seem to speak, it is not I, about me, it is not me' (p. 7). Starting with such shifting paradoxes, the narrator foresees that he can proceed only by way of doubting and ambiguity: 'by aporia pure and simple'. Of course there is nothing particularly pure or simple about *aporia*, a word whose meaning the narrator characteristically claims not to know. 'Aporia' is a keyword here. An old term given new currency in the critical jargon of our time (by the French deconstructionists and their followers), it can refer both to a style (a rhetorical figure) that shows that the speaker *doubts*, and to a method that discovers an impasse, or near-impossibility, in reaching a solution. No style and method could suit Beckett's present purpose better. The reader is warned, by a new philosophically dyed version of Sterne's sceptical and teasing narrator, not to trust the ignorant or impotent narrator: 'I shall have to speak of things of which I cannot speak.' Thus we have an early, 'logical' elimination of logic, in particular of the pre-modern narrative logic anchored to expectations of a stable narrator at the centre of the whole text. Once again a deeply felt questioning of thought, language and the self, is couched in the form of a quasi-philosophical inquiry and a parodied self-undermining novel.

The preamble attempts to define – even over-define – the narrator's present situation which he (let us assume that a male voice is speaking) despairs of being able to define. Almost every statement is immediately or soon negated, as in 'I shall not be alone, in the beginning. I am of course alone.' The second statement accords best with the narrator's situation in the microcosm of the text. No more encounters here – neither the mythic-picaresque kind still experienced by Molloy, nor the rare visitations or hallucinations of Malone. This narrator does appear to be ultimately isolated, but in total solitude his consciousness still spins words and images which throw up figments. At first these come from the preceding fiction, instanced by Malone. (Unless he is, after all, 'Molloy wearing Malone's hat', p. 9.) Then new figures begin to emerge, vague and inchoate ('It is no doubt time I gave a companion to Malone', p. 12), presumably springing from the Unnamable's struggle to create new fiction(s). It is difficult to doubt – amid all the doubting – that what is being projected here is the writer's consciousness caught in a verbal no-man's land: between the not yet wholly absent figures from the previous fiction and the not yet created but already foreshadowed (and very shadowy) new figures of a fiction to be written. At an imagined mid-point, somewhere between the discarded and not yet created personae, the speaking 'I' ('me alone', no longer Malone or his companion) is trying to emerge; compare the two following extracts:

All these Murphys, Molloys and Malones do not fool me. They have made me waste my time, suffer for nothing, speak of them when, in order to stop speaking, I should have spoken of me and of me alone. (p. 19)

. . . when I think of the time I've wasted with these bran-dips, beginning with Murphy . . . when I had me . . .   (p. 108)

On the existential level, the narrator thus finds himself in the tragicomic situation of an author who thinks he has wasted time on writing a many-volume saga while all along he wanted to write something else, his autobiography. But the undertone of irony points to a deeper sense of tragic waste – stretching backward and forward in time, without end. For in the fictional world of the narrator every new character/story about to be created turns into a NOT I, like all the past fictions. As we shall see, the language itself plunges the narrator into an alien world, and a 'successful autobiography' – that cliché – would itself be a fiction that falsifies the self. One escape from this dire predicament of the narrator seems to be myth, which projects the failing creative voice into something like a fallen angel, a failed demigod, on a cosmic scale:

> I am Matthew and I am the angel, I who came before the cross, before the sinning, came into the world, came here. (p. 17)

Elsewhere the narrator evokes Prometheus, who 'was delivered twenty-nine thousand nine hundred and seventy years after having purged his offence' (with an ironic denial of self-comparison, p. 19), and Lucifer:

> Hell itself, although eternal, dates from the revolt of Lucifer. It is therefore permissible, in the light of the distant analogy, to think of myself as *here for ever* but not as having been here forever.
>
> (p. 12, emphasis added)

Hell is a recurrent 'place' in the mythology of Beckett, though in other respects purgatory is the appropriate analogy, the 'proper place' for the self stripped of most attributes of the world. The suffering in this place, though apparently continuous and everlasting, is not necessarily intense. In the beginning, the narrator is anaesthetised ('devoid of feeling'), and yet his tears are streaming ('perhaps it is liquified brain', p. 9). Let us assume that, despite his sublime or abject detachment, the narrator is compassionately aware of the world's general sadness, which the Romans called *lacrimae rerum*. Yet when a feeble cry is heard, in the silence of this abandoned place, the narrator mocks his own elegiac tone: 'Is it not perhaps a simple little fart, they can be rending?' (p. 12)

The mythic pattern keeps recurring in the tapestry of words that speak of the Unnamable's extreme condition. Indeed it would be difficult to suggest an 'extreme condition' without a near-mythic imagery, since the endless monologue lacks the dramatic and 'clawingly' concrete imagery of *Molloy* and *Malone Dies*, or of the plays. Whenever the narrator attempts to report the particulars of his present condition, something like the contours of infinity are being outlined – akin to a creation myth, for a degenerate creation, as in *Endgame*. Concerning the place: it is vast ('as it may well measure twelve feet in diameter'), with pits, perhaps vertically layered, 'the place where one finishes vanishing' (p. 9). Grey opaque light (later turning black) commands the air; but from the fixed position of the narrator there is 'nothing to be seen, 99 per cent of the time' (p. 17) – his vision is limited to the phenomena immediately before him and 'what I best see I see ill' (p. 13). This myopic yet strangely privileged vision (comparable to the inarticulate yet highly articulate voices) is imitated by the form of the main text which follows: the endless unwinding of a spiral of phenomena not held in place firmly by a narrative frame.

Occupying the centre ('but nothing is less certain', p. 11), the narrator is seated, as he has *always* been. All the ideas he has received about the world of men had come from 'delegates' (another name for the *they* voices who constantly appear to dictate to the Beckettian narrator, sometimes like messengers from an unwanted Almighty with residual powers, sometimes resembling characters, like Basil). It is 'they' who have inculcated in this narrator the few general ideas he has – of good and evil, of his mother, and 'the low-down on God' (p. 14). In short, the narrator presents himself as no longer and not yet a person, fixed in a perpetually opaque void, with ideas not his own but carried by words spoken by alien if not hostile voices; he could do with a new language, one 'with future and conditional participles', (p. 16). In the meantime, a 'true voice', that of the not yet named speaker/writer, is trying to emerge.

Given such a strategy, *The Unnamable* is necessarily difficult to read. On top of the self-contradicting narrative – the devices of an impasse – there is the extreme fluidity of writing, a stream of overlapping motifs. Then there is the typographical (but also semantic) reading challenge set by the absence of paragraphing for the whole text after the preamble, and the replacement of sentences by rhythmic breath groups within the marathon ending. The reader is then forced to make up the chapters and episodes so to speak: to segment the work as well as establish its overall design. That may sound like a tall order. Yet the language of the novel will communicate its exhilarating power (it is much nearer to our communicative experience and less wilfully experimental than the language of Joyce's *Finnegans Wake*) provided we learn to read through the elements of 'unreadability' just outlined. In practice, every reader must work out an appropriate tempo of reading along with a gradually emerging and cumulative interpretation, with the maximum suspension of disbelief, and of belief (ideology) as well.

Such readings inform the present critical commentary too. It is necessarily selective in following the contours of an 'as if' narrative in the work, while trying to render its spiralling, constantly recurring and inter-connecting voices. The selective emphasis is to be on certain nodal points of the text, units that can be demarcated, which carry a major theme (diminishment, the quest for the self, the struggle for both utterance and silence, for instance). Such passages invariably display some distinctive narrative or stylistic device (devices which delay, interrupt, contradict, undermine and overlay the narration). As the two voices – self-reflection and endless meta-narratorial reflections on the text-in-the-making – are more seamlessly interwoven in *The Unnamable* than in the two previous novels of the trilogy, these planes of writing are not discussed here separately but rather as threaded utterances in a continuous discourse.

Total renunciation, only a voice remains (from 'I of whom I know nothing' . . . pp. 20 ff.). In a vigorous lament, not yet marked by the broken rhythm of the later laments, the narrator's voice personifies total dispossession. The cumulative symptoms of physical degeneration (spine not supported, nothing seen, the body reduced to the 'consistency of mucilage', deprived of a nose, of the genital organ, etc.) correspond to spiritual deprivation: 'mean words, and needless, from the mean old spirit' – no more God, and no more *pauses* either. This is just one of innumerable correspondences between diminished body, spirits, words and writing. The narrator is reduced to a 'talking ball, talking about things that do not exist'; nevertheless, the task of *speaking* remains, 'behind my mannikins' (p. 22), another synonym for the personae in the stories narrated. This otherwise non-specific task is called both 'lesson' and 'pensum' (the latter is, strictly speaking, a preparation for the lesson). Our initial hypothesis about the voice (that it is driven by the self-isolated writer's struggle with words) is further confirmed by its frustrated kicking against 'this futile discourse' – a discourse which may have to give way to another 'fairy-tale' (p. 23) or to 'the resources of fable', even though 'it might be better to keep on saying bababab, for example' (p. 24). Self-denigration then becomes inseparable from denigration of the work in progress; just as the self was born without willing itself, the work was begun as if through the agency of others, 'as a punishment for having been born perhaps' (p. 26). The compulsive element is underlined by the narrator's persistent murmuring against THEM, the THEY-voices (those pronouns for some slave-master), from now on sustained throughout the whole novel.

His master's relentless voice (from 'Well done, my child, well done, my son . . . My master. There is a vein I must not lose sight of' pp. 26 ff.). This super-voice is constantly evoked, though the narrator, as usual, cannot define it: there may be several commanding – yet ultimately powerless – voices: 'they', again, 'a college of tyrants', or 'deputies' (p. 29). They are akin to characters who, like Basil/Mahood, also dictate to the narrator. The little local father–son, master–servant dialogue that appears at this point is soon developed into a sustained mini-drama (pp. 28–30), giving voice to the master and in turn apostrophising 'him' ('I too, your Lordship. I say that to cheer him up, he sounds so unhappy.') Like Youdi in *Molloy* ('Moran's boss' is explicitly evoked), the master is reminiscent of a fallen deity, and is addressed in the inverted or mock-worshipful tone that is characteristic of an atheism haunted by religious language (like Hamm's failed prayer in *Endgame*). Indeed, the whole conception of obeying an unknown voice or listening to unknowable voices, has immediate mystical overtones, like much else in the trilogy. It also has affinities with the fictional world of Kafka, though Beckett always disrupts any cluster of quasi-religious images before they can crystallise into allegory. So in the end we don't even have a Pilgrim's Regress – only the voice of the Unnamable speaking of another source of voice(s), given provisional and parodied names, such as master.

The Mahood Stories (pp. 33–51, approximately). 'At the particular moment I am referring to, I mean when I took myself for Mahood, I must have been coming to the end of a world tour, perhaps not more than two or three centuries to go.' This sounds like the opening sentence of a story – a fantasy – asking the reader not to distinguish between the teller and the told, Mahood and the I-voice behind him. In the text as we have it, the story-telling situation is more complex than that, and it is deliberately blurred in the telling. For the Unnamable and Mahood are 'talking' in tandem ('if we are twain, as I say we are', p. 31): both in the first person, mostly in the present tense. The reader loses, then, those juxtapositions of memoir and story – with clear transitions from one to the other – which marked the almost classical structure of *Malone Dies*. Further, the I-voices of the teller (the Unnamable) and of the told (Mahood) are both unstable and they tend to get into each other's telling, entangled in two 'soft-edged' stories. Further still, the process of warming up for a story is prolonged and inevitably replete with reflective digressions. But here the linear conception of story-telling must itself be abandoned. The lines of the story-telling, within the Unnamable's own endless story, form a spiral, once more 'imitating' the narrator's conscious situation:

> I had already advanced a good ten paces, if one may call them paces, not in a straight line I need hardly say, but *in a sharp curve*, which if I continued to follow it, seemed likely to restore me to my point of departure, or to one adjacent. I must have got embroiled in a kind of *inverted spiral*, I mean one the coils of which, instead of widening more and more, grew narrower and narrower and finally . . . would come to an end for lack of room. (pp. 32–3 emphasis added)

These images – 'sharp curve', 'inverted spiral' – exactly catch not only the narrator's static situation but also the 'lines' of narration. Ironically – with a deliberate mocking echo of the vocabulary of a journey – he can still use words like 'advance', 'continued to follow' and 'world tour' (in the quotation that heads this section), suggesting the illusion of forward movement, traditional narrative. And when the narrator finally begins to tell his first story, it has echoes of the picaresque journey which provided the narratorial backbone for *Molloy*. For the first Mahood is depicted as a Wanderer, on crutches, a degenerate Ulysses figure who is on his way to visit his family only to find all of them exterminated by botulinus poisoning. He rejoices at the sight of the massacre and in the final, grotesquely parodic version (for there are several versions, with built-in stops for checking the 'true' version) the local epic hero boasts of stamping under foot the corpses of his family – 'it was in mother's entrails I spent the last days of my long voyage . . . Isolde's breast would have done just as well, or papa's private parts, or the heart of one of the little bastards' (p. 40). This Rabelaisian canvas is intersected by thin veins of the narrator's abstract reflections ('What they all wanted . . . was that I should exist' (p. 39), that is, exist through seeming to act, being witnessed and narrated, if only in this form of travesty.)

Between the first and the second Mahood stories the static narrator is duly returned to his reflexive fixity: 'I was never anywhere but here, no one ever got me out of here.' In a recurrent phrase significant for the whole novel, he laments that he has 'no language but theirs' (p. 42) and then takes refuge in the second Mahood, a parody of fixity *in extremis* which evokes the pathos of cruel suffering denied to the first Mahood and also (through many long sections of his solipsistic monologue) to the Unnamable. The story of this Mahood – 'stuck like a sheaf of flowers in a deep jar' (pp. 43 ff.) – is the only Malone-like, vividly concrete, imagistic and immediate episode in the novel. It is probably the source of some of Beckett's most memorable static-dramatic stage metaphors: the characters stuck in dustbins or in urns (in plays that also have something of the tonality of the limbo-world of *The Unnamable*). Not surprisingly, the second Mahood story has been anthologised and dramatised until it has become one of the best-known passages in Beckett's fiction, and it requires no further critical commentary here. In our context it will be noticed that the physical deprivations or mutilations of Mahood present yet another analogue to the spiritual deprivations of the narrator: 'I have dwindled, I dwindle', calls out the narrator as he is sinking towards the bottom of the jar (p. 47). Again there is a virtual fusion of the I-voices of the narrator/narrated, and the Mahood story itself dwindles around the diminishing remains of the self (as the far more shadowy figure of Worm is beginning to emerge).

The insubstantial presence of Worm. 'But it's time I gave this solitary a name, nothing doing without proper names. I therefore baptise him Worm. I don't like it, but I haven't much choice. It will be *my name too*, when the time comes, when I needn't be called Mahood any more . . . (pp. 54 ff. emphasis added). This rather puzzling introduction to what sounds like a new 'character', must be seen in the context of the narrator's voice fusing with that of (any) character – and refusing clear and distinct borders between different levels of fiction. Worm is an intensification of that peculiar 'grey area' or darkness where narrator and narrated dwell before being properly conceived. It is an intensification, for Worm is not even a voice, only a silent presence, a name and *nothing* but a name, pending the discovery of a proper name for the narrator. It is an elaborate parody of the writing process – at its most solitary or solipsistic. In this connection we may recall that Beckett's first title for this novel was 'Mahood' – and the title we have was arrived at later, presumably in the process of writing, through discovering a narrator who always eludes his true identity, his 'proper name'. Briefly Basil, then Mahood (= Manhood?) takes his place and gives the I-voice of the narrator a temporary and surrogate name (persona), only to be replaced, arbitrarily, by Worm (the serpent). This process could go on – Worm could give way to a certain Jones, for example – in an infinite series, without any promise that towards the end the true self/name of the Unnamable may be reached. Meanwhile, despite his desperate situation, the narrator is having fun with his predicament: apostrophising his new alter ego: 'Worm, Worm, it's between the three of us now and the devil take the hindmost' (p. 56), and dismissing Mahood (as Prospero dismisses his agents in *The Tempest*): 'The stories of Mahood are ended. He realised they could not be about me, he has abandoned [*sic*] it is I who win, who tried so hard to lose' . . . (p. 62).

Worm to play, his lead (pp. 63 ff.). However, Worm does not play, still less lead, in the world of this novel. As already suggested, he never crystallises into a speaking character anchored to story, image or concrete fictional setting. Indeed, right from the opening move of 'Worm to play', the narrator has despaired of Worm as another (an-*other*) potential character – 'the anti-Mahood' who might become an aid in self-discovery, a 'step towards me'. (The character's function almost certainly includes that of witnessing the existence of the Unnamable as narrator. This idea keeps recurring in Beckett: as in the philosophy of Berkeley, to be seen or observed is a proof of one's existence; while Sartre held that only another (person) can mediate between inner consciousness and outer reality.) The narrator's failure to create a new character finds expression in an increasingly paradoxical despair, in increasingly strained language:

To think I saw in him, if not me, a step towards me! To get me to be he, the anti-Mahood, and then to say, But what am I doing but living, in a kind of way, the only possible way, that's the combination. Or by the absurd prove to me that I am, the absurd of not being able. [*sic*]

Just as the narrator cannot be named, Worm cannot be known, and in the midst of abstract reflections, Worm is evoked as 'the all-impotent, all-nescient'. This sounds like an inversion, and a parody, of the traditional attributes of God. But the language also has echoes of the 'negative way' of the mystics (*via negativa*), who tried to reach God through non-definition, not naming, and even through denial. So here, around the very name of the shadowy Worm, a litany of 'nothings' is recited, including an analogy between this would-be character and 'us': 'the one outside of life we always were in the end, all our long vain life long'. The underlying analogy here as elsewhere is between *being* and *writing*: impotent human beings, like unformed characters, in face of an impotent author (Creator?).

The extreme scepticism towards, or renunciation of, existence and creation (writing) is explored – around the mere name of Worm – in an ever more winding and repetitive monologue (over forty pages, making up the second part of the novel before the sustained final lament). Here we find a ceaseless variation on themes already well-rotated in the preamble, in the opening monologue, and in the Mahood stories. Admittedly the extreme dispossession of Worm takes the self's inner nakedness to a further intensity, often in a still vigorous prose style. Even so, by this stage the combination of length, density, lack of concreteness and the hypnotic multiple repetition/variation/incantation of known themes, has produced a very 'problematic' text. The systematic 'imitation' of diminishment and failure, pushes the writing itself towards painfully self-conscious failure. Well beyond all the previous parodies of fiction, we now have a constant self-parody of *this text*, this moment of writing. So the reader's interest may well focus increasingly on the authorial patter, sharp and witty in flashes, in an otherwise tired reiteration of the exhaustion of the writer. The 'meta-writing' becomes inseparable from the writing. Here the growing despair over the shackling limitations of language predominates – the inadequacy of personal pronouns, tenses, punctuation and finally *all language*.

The narrator's inability to find a name for that incessantly speaking voice is the source of a general uncertainty about all naming. As nearly all personal utterance is anchored to a central 'I am' in our culture, in our grammar of statements (see also p. 128 above), it is perilous for a writer to embark on a monologue hinging on an I-voice that is fundamentally unstable and discontinuous: 'there is no name for me, no pronoun for me' (p. 122). So when the monologue has shed nearly all its narrative functions – in the Worm story that is not a story – a sudden pronoun shift is announced with a sense of desperate triumph:

I shall not say I again, ever again, it's too farcical. I shall put in its place, whenever I hear it, the third person, if I think of it. Anything to please them. It will make no difference. (p. 72)

And it does not 'make a difference', for the obsessional themes, the syntax, the vocabulary and the rhythm of utterances does not change. (This foreshadows the much more desperate drama of Mouth, the woman or female voice that could not bring herself to tell the story of a wasted life in the first person in *Not I*, 1973). After nine pages the 'I'-voice returns ('But not too fast, it's too soon to return, to where I am', p. 81), to alternate thereafter with the third person. When the 'I'- voice returns once more (p. 85), it is even more intense, as if speaking at a higher pitch, more breathlessly, as it approaches the final lament. Shifts of tense also occur, sometimes inconspicuously, sometimes underlined: 'For my face reflects . . . It is true my mouth was hidden . . . Ah yes, sometimes it's in the past, sometimes in the present' (p. 44). Equally significant are the style-conscious remarks which parody the text now being written and which become, appropriately, more frequent as the speaker's language pains increase:

'But why keep on saying the same thing?' (p. 70)
'But let us close this parenthesis and, with a light heart, open the next'
(p. 71)
'Perhaps I've missed the keyword to the whole business' (p. 86)
'Gaps, there have always been gaps, it's the voice stopping it's the voice failing to carry me' (p. 86)
'for the words don't carry any more' (p. 87, early in that long litany on words which leads into the prolonged conclusion)

From time to time the strong black humour of the earlier fiction is recovered: 'the alleviations of flight and self' is compared to 'the hussar who gets up on a chair the better to adjust the plume of his busby' (p. 85). The monotony is celebrated, or the need for breaking it is dramatised: 'But a little animation now for pity's sake, it's now or never, a little spirit, it won't produce anything, not a budge, that doesn't matter, we are not trades-men' (p. 88). The endless repetition within a spiralling structure is likewise dramatised by the entrance – in a text that has no typographical breaks – of the endless round 'A dog crawled into a kitchen'

(p. 96; Vladimir is to sing this round at the beginning of Act II in *Waiting for Godot*).

This spiralling, 'endless' form – imitating the slow/rapid/slow final progression or regression in the voice – then becomes the vehicle for the final virtuoso confession of the Unnamable. In the pages leading up to this finale (roughly from 'And now one last look at Mahood, at Worm', p. 97, to 'The Words are everywhere', p. 104), the diminishing and indefinable voice is still attempting to define itself, in vigorous self-parody: 'a sperm dying, of cold in the sheets, feebly wagging its little tail, perhaps I'm a drying sperm, in the sheets of an innocent boy, even that takes time' (p. 97). The parody is countered by the pathos of total uncertainty and insubstantiality: *'perhaps it's not a voice at all*, perhaps it's the air, ascending, descending, flowing, eddying, seeking exit, finding none' (p. 99, emphasis added). In a further intensification of this feeling of utter physical and spiritual weightlessness, the voice that has come to doubt even its being a voice (in extreme paradox it 'says' that it is speaking without a mouth) hits on the new idea that it may be just the 'partition' between 'inside' and 'outside':

I'm the partition, I've two surfaces and no thickness, perhaps that's what I feel, myself vibrating, I'm the tympanum, on the one hand the mind, on the other the world, I don't belong to either. (p. 100)

The Unnamable began by getting dispossessed of time past and future, of space as extension, of a name (as focus of a stable consciousness linked to circumstance and identity, body and movement); it went through the very much more painful process of dispossessing itself of the pronoun 'I' (yet failing to become 'not I'); towards the end it is in the process of losing its voice even while it is still 'in voice'. It goes on still, if not exactly speaking, then issuing a stream of words, for it is, inescapably, *made of words*. The language is, then, the final unsheddable bondage, which cannot be silenced, yet:

I'm in words, made of words, others' words, what others, the place too, the air, the walls, the floor, the ceiling, all words, the whole world is here with me, I'm the air, the walls, the walled-in-one, everything yields, opens, ebbs, flows, like flakes.   (p. 104)

This sounds like yet another metaphor for the extreme situation of the solitary self/writer reduced to a verbal universe (versions of which we have discussed earlier). But at this point even the

151

metaphoric presentation of such an extreme state becomes secondary, and a form of rhythmic and incantatory 'confession' becomes primary. It is possible to get the 'vision' only by submitting to the 'form': this symphonic prose of nearly thirty pages which has a cumulative, at times hypnotic effect. It could be analysed in detail, it could even be submitted to a computer count of its repetition of keywords . . . But it is not necessary, or desirable, to do so, for the final breathless marathon of this novel communicates directly through its verbal rhythms. It may well be best to listen to it first on one of the recordings made (such as the excellent reading by Patrick Magee with music by John Beckett), or else to read aloud substantial sections. The new intensity of this panting rhythm – based on staccato breath groups which carry fragments of the leading themes that have been sounded from the preamble on – does release a cumulative meaning. It is a meaning that is not primarily conceptual, but it is not obscure. The by-and-large simple vocabulary, the ceaseless repetition of now familiar themes and motifs, especially the haunting obsession with three things – 'the inability to speak, the inability to be silent, and solitude' (p. 114) – form the sense-base for a new kind of writing. It is a further intensification or mutation of what the whole trilogy has been about. The main struggle is that of the 'dying voice' (like an inward counterpart of the dying Malone) translating itself into that new rhythm. Meanwhile, the fictionalising goes on, there is even a final miniature 'love-story', sandwiched into the self-undermining finale (pp. 124–5). Before the ending, a new method of writing through words as 'fundamental sounds' is worked out – the first example of a verbal technique further developed in Beckett's later works, both in the fiction and in the plays from *Play* on. And the final words of the Unnamable – 'I can't go on, I'll go on' – may be heard as the authorial voice behind the voice of the Unnamable, repeatedly sounded in the later works, always trying to go silent but then inescapably speech-ridden by that rhythmic movement of words.

III
CONCLUSION

11

Concluding reflections

This book inevitably carries the traces of pressure, of both contemporary and personal points of awareness. Beckett's work has now reached an all but universal public and is met with increasing receptivity. One can even speak of the growing popularity of Beckett though not without certain ironies. The feeling that Beckett 'speaks to our condition' must help the reception of his work; but, at the same time, the 'culture gap' between dominant aspects of the contemporary world and Beckett's world also appears to be growing. The spiritual and linguistic complexity of Beckett (with its roots in modernism, as we have argued) comes into collision, at certain points, with a brasher, at once more superficial and more technological 'post-modernist' culture (a somewhat ill-defined term for literature, used here only as a pointer). Whilst our culture is seemingly hurtling in much more extroverted directions, a new generation of readers and theatre-goers is attuned – probably more than the immediate post-war generation was – to the inward and unstable elements in Beckett's work: its spirit of uncertainty, humility and fundamental scepticism. At the same time, an age that no longer regards realistic 'representation' as the norm of writing is likely to be more receptive to radical artistic experimentation to the very limits of writing.

While Beckett is decelerating, as it were, the circus around him is accelerating. For example, Beckett's writing – with its delicate placing of the shades and echoes of words – is often drafted in long-hand and meticulously re-worked in hand-corrected typescripts, (many of the holographs and typescripts can be seen at the Beckett Archive of Reading University), while our word-processor-equipped literary institutions increasingly view writing itself as a quantifiable production, subject to market research, strict page-counting and highly simplified types of publicity. Simultaneously, the accelerating momentum of academic criticism – another multinational industry – is 'processing' Beckett's work at a speed unprecedented in former times. (We may contrast the time that was needed, a generation ago, for the gradual growth of a critical literature around a living writer – Joyce, Lawrence, Virginia Woolf, even Eliot.) Yet a reader, certainly a first reader, needs to respond to the words – and the silences – of a Beckett text with full attention, empathy and stillness, *before* being exposed to the conceptualising urgencies and jargon of certain types of commentary which sometimes mime (in one of Lucky's phrases) the 'labours . . . crowned by the Acacacacademy of Anthropopopometry'. On the other hand, criticism needs to avoid virtual identification with its subject – turning Beckett as writer into a cult figure. Fortunately, a considerable number of Beckett critics *have* managed to avoid the dual dangers of over-conceptualisation and cultism; and Beckett's work has been illuminated, in three decades, by a body of scholarship and interpretation which has itself become a substantial context for reading the texts.

This study is aware of that context, but has aimed at working back to, and from, the texts and performances as primary experiences: their quickening, pre-conceptual impact, in a series of salutary shocks, as Beckett's work unfolded itself – in the present writer's experience starting with the first London production of *Waiting for Godot*.

All reflection at this stage is guided by the overriding question: what can be seen in sharper focus from the present perspective? First, it is clear that Beckett's work has an underlying consistency, an inner coherence – its artistry is guided by a single-minded vision, as if driven by inner voices, 'demons'. Six decades of sustained writing, now approaching the end, is itself an astonishing feat of creativity to set against the myth of 'failure' – failure of self and of words – which has served Beckett as private poetics. Such a long creative life (which Beckett did not expect) inevitably brings repetitions of theme across the continuously varied forms of innovation: the same intense questions keep revolving in and around the isolated and unnamable voice – and keep finding other voices that struggle with a self-engulfing language.

What we have called vision is, insistently, visionary – as in Dante, Bunyan, Blake or Kafka, those allegorists of the human spirit, shapers of mythologies. Again and again, particularly in the plays, the vision becomes directly visual (we saw how in *Happy Days* all reflection and verbal complexity hinged on the simple presence of the almost buried body of Winnie). This power to visualise – to create stage metaphors – may give the plays greater artistic power than all but the most fully achieved novels (the first part of *Molloy* and *Malone Dies*). In the fiction, removed from the immediate 'presence' of stage metaphor, the reader is involved in the endless verbalisations of 'absence'. When a unifying theme (such as the quest) is abandoned or vaporised, all the energy goes into the whirling self-consciousness of the act of writing, which reveals a writer behind the writer in a kind of infinite regress. A novel like *The Unnamable*, with all its insights, may never attain the lasting universality of, for example, Kafka's *The Castle*, where images of a fragmented human condition are not yet further refracted by the internal mirrors of the word-seeking self. In some respects, as in the late texts (see below) Beckett has taken fiction to such naked exploration of inner voices that future writing can take it no further (just as Joyce's *Finnegans Wake*, in its gigantic ambition, has proved to be an inimitable dead end in the evolution of the novel). At the same time, the plays have already transformed our whole conception of Western drama and theatre. It is hard now even to imagine their eclipse – as the once celebrated plays of Maeterlinck (1862–1949) have virtually vanished from our stages. They are likely to remain living and significant as plays in the theatre – hence our emphasis on their theatricality – whether or not they are to have a lasting *direct* influence on younger dramatists. Such influence was over-eagerly sought by critics in the decade after *Godot*, for example in the very different texture of Pinter's plays. However, two decades later there are distinct signs of many contemporary dramatists swinging once more towards a more referential and world-mirroring theatre.

Wherever we look in Beckett's drama and fiction, we see images of spiritual loss, and of human suffering and waste. To call such a vision 'pessimistic' or 'nihilistic' is facile unless its complexity and many contrary impulses, are registered and felt. A profound sense of loss pervades all Beckett's work, quite distinct from the glib contemporary casualness towards certain states of diminishment – 'the death of God', the prolonged agony of de-creation. Where there is negation there is also ambivalence or double vision: a constant evocation of buried values (or of no longer usable bicycles, crutches, painkillers, quotations, which are being used all the same), fragments of the 'old style' charged with religious, moral and existential overtones. The agnostic probing of former certainties is itself sorrowful, and haunted by a memory of lost values and styles. A compassionate and humane awareness frames even the recurrent images of violence, sadism and cruelty, starting with Pozzo's whip for Lucky and Molloy hammering on his mother's skull. And even the extreme apocalyptic images of *Endgame* are shot through with tragicomic humour ('There's no more nature.' / 'No more nature! You exaggerate.') Performance of the plays brings laughter; and the reading of most of the texts is accompanied by local fits of mirth. The haunted, melancholy voices tend also to be accompanied by a paradoxically intrepid, stoical, voice – Sisyphus inexplicably persisting on rolling his stone (as in the otherwise different vision of Camus), with variations on the text of 'I can't go on, I must go on.'

It follows from these reflections that I do not think that the value of Beckett's work can be reduced by the kind of moral criticism that once dismissed the novels of Joyce while exclusively praising the life-affirming and 'natural' fiction of D. H. Lawrence. The vitality of Beckett's writing, his concern with a living yet chastened language, as well as the humour and humanity just mentioned, should be enough to warn off over-confident users of succulent adjectives such as 'dead', 'artificial' or 'decadent'. Orthodox Marxist criticism – with its insistence that literature should reflect our world as a lived, multi-layered, historical reality – has tended to see Beckett as an ahistorical writer, dealing with only the 'timeless' aspects of 'the human situation' and unconcerned with social reality. But the social criterion of literature was itself narrowly thought out, for a literary work inescapably 'reflects' its social context even when it seems subjective, dream-spun, apolitical.[1] For the language itself carries the world – from the cosmos to the modern city – into the inner speech of the mind and into the texts: our language is dripping with rhetorical reflections of the world and in the end everything is named – even the unnamable. Further, Beckett's radical art and language may be said to have affinities with directly revolutionary attacks on the order of a 'patriarchal society'. Radical means reaching for the roots.

Attempts to highlight a programme, ideological or literary, in the body of Beckett's work, have proved reductive beyond the usual simplification of commentators dominated by an 'ism'. But then, somewhat paradoxically, one kind of reductive reading in our time comes from the seemingly friendly embrace of Beckett by those who would turn the instability of the self and of language – the experience of absence, impasse and uncertainty – into a doctrine. Then Beckett is glibly turned into an apostle of a new relativism where 'anything goes', in utterance as in writing. The elements of implicit 'deconstruction' in the trilogy (see chapter 6, esp. pp. 137–8, 141, 149ff.) were clearly worked into the text by Beckett with authentic human and artistic difficulty. Reading Beckett should make us humble rather than triumphantly certain that our uncertainties are new absolutes.

The pattern of gradual diminishment – repeatedly traced in this study – was not intended to be a thesis imposed on Beckett's work, but to follow the contours of that work. It should help us to see, at every level, the artistic consequences of Beckett's early choice of dispossesion. That pattern is like an inverted and tapering mountain – Beckett's own Mount Purgatory – with diminishing circles that end near a vanishing peak.

The works we have studied – in succession and in comparison – reveal a relentless if gradual compression, of fiction and play, of form and language. This pattern has been, if anything, understated or incompletely mapped out in our study. It would be even clearer if we studied the whole span of Beckett's work, from the Joycean writings of his youth to the miniature texts of his old age. The work of the thirties, written in English (of which *Proust* and *Murphy* are our only examples) is often extravagantly rich in verbal patterning, situational inventiveness and 'clever' mannerism. After the great post-war pruning – when Beckett started writing in French and simultaneously turned his back on remnants of realism – the word-flood abates, though it re-emerges in appropriate places: in the picaresque and lyrical sections of the trilogy, often through parody and pastiche, and in the exaggerated stage rhetoric of characters like Pozzo and Hamm, those ham actors. The richness is also there in the radio play *All That Fall* (1957), which has surreal/real Irish local colour woven into a verbal tapestry, a unique example of that kind in Beckett's work. Later, the vocabulary, though not the texture of words, becomes simpler, as in *Happy Days*. The main thrust is towards greater purity and a sustained withdrawal from the 'titanic' heritage of learning and language, paralleled by the withdrawal from the created world and the remnants of self. It is continuous growth through 'lessness'. The price Beckett pays for this development – in keeping with the doctrine of continuous innovation – includes the abandonment of what has just been achieved. For instance, the supreme counterpoint of concrete and abstract writing achieved in *Malone Dies* for fiction, and *Happy Days* for drama, was all too soon abandoned, and never to be repeated, for the sake of a further descent into limbo/hell – and into a further, more abstract and more intense rhythmic incantation – in the final sequences of the *The Unnamable* and in *Play*.

In this selective study these two works mark the furthest points of 'lessening' in fiction and drama respectively. But in Beckett's total work the process of refinement and compression has gone on, towards the highly compressed monologue, the short fiction and drama of inner voices. In over two decades, 'grain upon grain', a substantial heap of these 'minimalist' texts has accumulated: fiction from *Imagination Dead Imagine* (1965, the first one to be published, though not the first written), and play-texts from *Not I* (1972), in which Mouth, the suffering old woman, is condemned to soliloquise incessantly without ever being able to utter the pronoun 'I'. Taken together, these texts constitute a significant period in Beckett's work, and some of them are radically new departures which are likely to be for all time. Their artistic inventiveness is very varied, even though they may suggest rows of narrowing windows closing upon increasingly inward worlds – the bone-bound territory of a weary brain, aptly called 'frescoes of the skull'.[2] The old theme of making an end (as in *Endgame* and *The Unnamable*) recurs through variations, as fading voices go on rehearsing that old theme: 'Weaker still the weak old voice that tried in vain to make me, dying away as much as to say it's going from here to try elsewhere . . .' (*Texts for Nothing* XIII, written as long ago as 1950, in *No's Knife* (1967), p. 133). With conscious irony Beckett has given belittling titles to several texts, expecially when collected (*For to End Yet Again and Other Fizzles* (1970, 1976); *Ends and Odds* (1977); *Six Residua* (1977)), or punning titles that parody one of his own obsessive themes (*Lessness* (1970) and *Worstward Ho* (1983)).

Most of these works require repeated and very attentive close reading (which is one reason why the publishers felt that a proper study of the late fiction and drama would go beyond the aims and scope of this book). In the present context, these texts confirm the inseparability of 'form' and 'vision' for Beckett, in their pursuit of still more radical ventures into the unknown, into final solitude or solipsism and into 'lessness'.

In form, these works may well be seen as the furthest examples of that expression beyond expression which Beckett first adumbrated in his dialogues on painters (see Introduction, pp. 14–15). They spring from that old avant-gardist urge which, beginning with the symbolists, has wanted literature to be an approximation to music and, more recently, to non-figurative painting. This urge is based on a partial fallacy, since language – 'the dialect of the tribe' – can never be purified to the point where syntax and 'ordinary language' leave no trace in the writing. Beckett is implicitly aware of this, hence the persistent struggle with 'the words that remain', a struggle that reaches a self-destructive dimension in *The Unnamable*. The stronger the obsession with words, the stronger the urge to escape from them.

Beckett, like Joyce, has always been haunted by words as 'fundamental sounds'; and in the late texts the aural patterning is intensified, as earlier in *The Unnamable*, in *How It Is* and in *Play*, which all foreshadow the textures of the late work. In the plays a panting rhythm calls for a wholly new type of speaking voice – a new and strenuous challenge to the actor, as we know from the testimony of Billie Whitelaw and others who have worked with Beckett in the theatre. In the fiction, those voices call for reading aloud so that the breath-groups become first audible and then visible in print (several texts have unpunctuated and unparagraphed typography). Broadcast versions have helped to familiarise many of these texts,[3] bringing out their hidden vocal power, varied rhythms, and silences. Like certain compressed compositions – late Stravinsky and Webern – the texts require re-play.

Almost as strong is the visual patterning, the drive towards equivalents of abstract painting – quite different from the strongly pictorial and figurative images of the mature work (those dustbins and urns, the self-portraits of Molloy and Malone, or even Mahood 'stuck like a sheaf of flowers in a deep jar'). For example, 'whiteness' recurs as an all-embracing, infinite, colourless colour: 'all white in the whiteness the rotunda . . . Lying on the ground two white bodies . . . White too the vault . . . white in the whiteness' (*Imagination Dead Imagine*, pp. 7–8 (1965)). The body is again 'white on whiteness invisible' in *Ping* (1966); and the remnants of a landscape, moorland with sheep, become just 'white splotches in the grass' in *Ill Said Ill Seen* (p. 11). That movement towards life-lessness, 'that white speck lost in whiteness' (in the close of *Imagination* like the shades of darkness in *Company* (1980)) may be compared to the countless modernist paintings (starting with

Malevitch) of a white square upon a white background. These invite the onlooker to meditation, to a quasi-mystical experience of 'as if' figures perceived where there are no figures. It is one of the forms religion may take in an age without faith. (Once again we recall Beckett's writings on painters in 'Three Dialogues' and elsewhere – see also p. 14). The drive towards verbal abstraction can also be seen in the device of permutations for word clusters: ringing the changes of a dozen words, in a solemn procession of twenty-four paragraphs in *Lessness*, or in the ritual repetition of a non-dictionary word like 'ping' (in the text so named) offering a bold 'new language' that is, inescapably, still leaning on the sounds, the meanings and the grammar we know.

Yet it would be wrong to over-stress the elements of abstraction. For Beckett always returns to 'the human form divine', or rather the human form no longer so divine as it was in Blake's vision. There is an ineluctable concern with the person, particularly in some of the texts written in the eighties, where the difficulties of extreme experimentation (permutational and graphological) are given up for the sake of the simpler voices of memory. These voices have recognisable (that is, no longer disguised) autobiographical accents, as in the three-threaded voices of one man's three ages in the short play *That Time* (1976), and in the consummate short fiction (a good starting point for the late work) *Company*. There the isolated writer/speaker, lying on his back in a dark place, discovers (he cannot be certain) that he may not be alone, that he may not be writing for/speaking to self alone:

Yet another then. Of whom nothing. Devising figments to temper his nothingness. [. . .]
Devised deviser devising it all for company. (p. 64)

All the fictionalising (the figments, the 'lying') includes a search for that other voice or person who – in Beckett's fiction – is as unattainable as the true core of the self. We recognise in this the remnant of the old Platonic or Romantic longing for essences; for a further union of word and being, self and non-self. And it is probable that the Beckett world, for all its fundamental scepticism and drive towards 'nothingness', is guided by a much stronger remnant of those immortal longings – essence, union, communion, divinity – than are likely to be admitted by most of our contemporaries. More simply, the human urge for shared existence is glimpsed behind the urgencies of writing and talking, as if the solitary person were crying out for 'company' like the dying woman's confessional voice in *Rockaby* (1981):

time she went and sat
at her window
only window
facing other windows
other only windows
all eyes
all sides
high and low
for another
another like herself
a little like
another living soul
one other living soul

[*Together*: i.e. the speaking woman and the voice-over – *echo of 'living soul', coming to rest of rock, faint fade of light. Long Pause.*]

Collected Shorter Plays (London, 1984), pp. 277–8.

This rocking rhythm, fusing lullaby and dirge, is bound to end with a withdrawal into a final solitude, a cursing of life coupled with acceptance of its finality, 'the coming to rest of rock'. But before the end we glimpse the solitary self's constant need for talking, soliloquising: 'for another' . . . It is the counterpart of the solo voice splitting into a couple or a pseudocouple, into dialogue or the semblance of dialogue: 'the solitary child who turns himself into children, two, three, so as to be together, and whisper together, in the dark' (*Endgame*, p. 45). That solitary child – in countless versions of ageing and decay – may be heard as a primal source of the ceaseless writing which has created the self-mocking elegy of Beckett's total work.

Notes

Notes have been kept to the minimum and references are made only to a few essential secondary sources.

Introduction

1 The late texts, not discussed in detail, are essential for a true perspective of Beckett's total work. See Concluding reflections, ch. 11 this volume.
2 Quoted by Deirdre Bair, *Samuel Beckett: A Biography* (London, 1980), p. 22.
3 Eoin O'Brien, *The Beckett Country* (London, 1986).
4 Stephen in Joyce's *A Portrait of the Artist as a Young Man* (1916, rpt. London, 1956), p. 194: 'His language, so familiar and so foreign, will always be an acquired speech for me . . . My soul frets in the shadow of his language.' W. B. Yeats, *The Rose Leaf* (London, 1895), vol. 2, p. 166. *All that Fall* (London, 1957), pp. 31–2.
5 Artaud's 'theatre of cruelty' does not seem to have had a special appeal for Beckett.

1. Contexts for the plays

1 Ruby Cohn, *Just Play* (Princeton, 1980), pp. 143–72, 172.
2 [Proust] 'describes the radiographical quality of his observation. The copiable he does not see' *Proust* (1931, rpt. London, 1965), p. 83. See also earlier discussion of Beckett on Proust (pp. 8–9).
3 For the Irish connection see Katharine Worth, *The Irish Drama of Europe from Yeats to Beckett* (London, 1974); for the connection with the Japanese Noh drama see Yasunari Takahashi, 'The Theatre of Mind – Samuel Beckett and the Noh', in *Encounter*, April 1982. Both these authors have other very interesting published writing on their subjects. See also books listed under 'For further study', pp. 167–8.

2. *Waiting for Godot*

1 These interpretations are a modified version of those cited by Colin Duckworth in his introduction to *En attendant Godot* (London, 1966), p. xcviii.

NOTES

3. *Endgame*

1 'More inhuman than Godot', *Village Voice*, New York, 19 March 1958.
2 The Berlin production notes, based on Michael Haerdter, *Materialien zu Becketts 'Endspiel'* (Frankfurt, 1968) and *Modern Drama*, 29, no. 1 (March 1976), p. 27.

7. Contexts for the fiction

1 This saying of Guelincx – in Latin or Belgo-Latin: *ubi nihil vales, ibi nihil velis* – has haunted Beckett, presumably as much for its shape as its meaning. It is quoted in *Murphy* as well as in the story *The End*. Traditional as well as modern existentialist philosophy is a more direct context in the novels than in the plays, but the position stated in the general introduction – the ideas should be seen chiefly as 'fiction-engendering' material, pp. 3 and 9–10 – still applies.
2 Bair, *Samuel Beckett* (1980) p. 469.
3 The other novels before *Molloy* are: *Dream of Fair to Middling Women* (written in 1932 but not published until 1983), *Watt* (written in English in 1942–5, published 1953), and *Mercier and Camier* (written in French in 1946, published in English in 1974).

  Beckett also wrote four novella-sized stories before the trilogy (in 1945, first in French): *The Expelled*, *The Calmative*, *The End*, and *First Love*. The first three are available in *No's Knife* (London, 1967), the last title in a separate volume (published in English as late as 1973). Both *First Love* and *The End* could be read as an excellent light introduction to Beckett's fiction.

10. Concluding reflections

1 It was the Frankfurt critic Theodor Adorno who defended Beckett from the charge of not 'reflecting' our social world made by Lukács and other orthodox Marxist critics. (See my 'Lukács and Modern Literature' in *Critical Quarterly*, 21, no. 4 (1979) pp. 53–60, especially p. 57. The moral critics referred to earlier in the paragraph are, clearly, followers of F. R. Leavis.
2 James Knowlson and John Pilling, *Frescoes of the Skull: The Later Prose and Drama of Samuel Beckett* (London, 1979).
3 Most of these excellent recordings can be heard at the National Sound Archive of the British Library, South Kensington, London. Discography by James Knowlson in *Recorded Sound*, 85 (January 1984).

Select bibliography

Details of works discussed

These dates give the date of writing (F = French language text later translated into English by Beckett; no sign = written in English) followed by first publication and, for the plays, first production in Britain only. For full bibliographical information see C. George Sandulescu, *A Beckett Synopsis* in Clive Hart, *Language and Structure in Beckett's Plays* (London, 1986). For dates of publication or first performance of other principal works, see the chronology on p. xi–xiii.

Note: works preceding and following the texts under discussion are mentioned in the relevant introduction and in Concluding reflections.

Waiting for Godot – written in 1948–9 (F, *En attendant Godot*), first London publication: Faber 1956, first London performance: Arts Theatre Club, 3 August 1955. Note: the English text differs in some respects, and a comparison with the annotated edition of the French text by Colin Duckworth (see n. 1 of Chapter 2) is recommended.

Endgame – written 1955–6 (F, *Fin de partie*), first London publication: Faber 1958, first London productions: (in French) Royal Court Theatre, 3 April 1957, (in English) also at the Royal Court, 28 October 1958. No theatre in Paris was willing to put on this play at first. The play was originally intended to be in two acts.

Krapp's Last Tape – written 1957, first London publication: Faber 1958, first London performance: Royal Court Theatre, 28 October 1958 (i.e. a double bill with *Endgame*!).

Happy Days – written 1960–1, first London publication: Faber 1963, first London production: Royal Court Theatre, 1 November 1962.

Play – written 1962–3, first London publication: Faber 1964, first London performance: National Theatre at the Old Vic, 7 April 1964 (in a double bill with the *Philoctetes* of Sophocles).

Murphy – written 1938, first publication: Routledge, London 1938.

Molloy – written (F) 1951, first Paris publication: Editions de Minuit, 1951, first London publication: Calder 1959.

Malone Dies – written (F, *Malone Meurt*) 1948 (? according to Sandulescu), first Paris publication: Editions de Minuit, 1951, first London publication: Calder 1957.

The Unnamable – written (F, *L'Innommable*) 1953 (?), first Paris publication: Editions de Minuit, 1953, first London publication: Calder, 1958.

For further study

This classified list is suggested as appropriate further reading for students of this book, and is not intended to be comprehensive.

General studies

Ben-Zvi, Linda, *Samuel Beckett* (Boston, Mass., 1986) – A good comprehensive study, covering Beckett's total work (and so necessarily brief on texts).

Cohn, Ruby, *Back to Beckett* (Princeton, NJ, 1973) – A detailed and sympathetic commentary.

Coe, Richard N., *Samuel Beckett* (London and New York, 1964) – An early study that places a strong emphasis on Beckett's philosophical background.

Pilling, John, *Samuel Beckett* (London, 1976) – The fullest general study with possibly excess detail on Beckett's intellectual, cultural and literary background.

The plays

Fletcher, Beryl S. and John, *A Student's Guide to the Plays of Samuel Beckett* (London, 1978, rpt. 1985).

Fletcher, John, and Spurling, John, *Beckett: A Study of his Plays* (London, 1972).

Kennedy, Andrew K., *Six Dramatists in Search of a Language* (Cambridge, 1975), esp. chapter 3.

See also Introduction and Contexts for the plays for specific topics and works by Ruby Cohn, James Knowlson, Yasunari Takahashi and Katharine Worth.

The fiction

Abbott, H. Porter, *The Fiction of Samuel Beckett. Form and Effect* (Berkeley and London, 1973).

Fletcher, John, *The Novels of Samuel Beckett* (London, 1964).

Christensen, Inger, *The Meaning of Metafiction* (Oslo, 1981).

Scherzer, Dina, *Structure de la trilogie de Beckett* (The Hague, 1976).

Sheringham, Michael, *Beckett – Molloy* (London, 1985).

SELECT BIBLIOGRAPHY

The late works

Brater, Enoch, *Beyond Minimalism – Beckett's Late Style in the Theater* (New York and Oxford, 1987).
Knowlson, James and Pilling, John, *Frescoes of the Skull: The Later Prose and Drama of Samuel Beckett* (London 1979 and New York 1980).

Biography

Bair, Deirdre, *Samuel Beckett: A Biography* (London, 1980).

Reception

Cook, Virginia (compiler), *Beckett on File* (London and New York, 1985).
Graver, Lawrence and Federman, Raymond (eds.), *Samuel Beckett – The Critical Heritage* (London, 1979).

Index

Shakespearian echoes, 74
tape recorder, 2, 67
television production, 74
theatricality, 74
time, 68
and *Waiting for Godot*, 68
Koestler, Arthur, 10

landscape, Irish, 5–6
language, 2, 13, 158–61
Anglo-Irish, 5–6, 21
bilingualism, 4, 6, 10–11, 19
failure, sense of, 15
Finnegans Wake, 8, 11
and landscape, 6
philosophies of, 6
reinvigoration, 11
symbolism, 6, 12, 161
and Synge, 21
tragicomedy, 6–7
uncertainty, 14
see also individual texts
late texts, 1, 2–3, 13, 88, 128, 150,
160–3
and *Happy Days*, 23
and *Play*, 98
Laurel and Hardy, 5, 45
Lawrence, D. H., 156, 158
lessness, 1, 11, 104, 159
Lessness, 160, 162
Lloyd, Harold, 5

Maeterlinck, Maurice, 20, 66, 157
Magee, Patrick, 2, 74, 152
Malevitch, Kasimir, 161
Mallarmé, Stéphane, 12
Malone Dies, **125–138**, 157
act of writing, 130–1, 133
Balzac, 135
black humour, 126
Cartesian affirmation, 128
confinement, 125
Dedalus, Stephen, 6, 131
deconstruction, 138
diminishment, 105, 126, 129, 131, 132
137–8
and *Endgame*, 126
games, 126
immobility, 125

and Joyce, 131
as memoir, 106, 125, 130
metaphysical poetry, 128
and *Molloy*, 125, 129, 132
novel parody, 134
setting, 5, 6, 126, 128–9, 130
soul-searching, 127–8
stories, 130, 131–8, 139
structure, 131–2
style, 159–60
and Swift, 127
time, 129, 132–3
Unnamable, The, 128, 139–41, 146,
147, 152
Waiting for Godot, 126, 127
Mann, Thomas, 106
Marxism, 7
Marxist criticism, 31, 158
Masson, André, 14
Mauthner, Fritz, 6
McGovern, Barry, 125
melodrama, 20, 35
Merry Widow, The, 81, 86
metaphysical poetry, 128
modernism, 2, 7, 11–12, 14, 32, 47,
112, 155
Molloy, 56, **109–24**, 157, 158
authorial, intervention, 120–1
and Dante, 113–14, 119
diminishment, 117–18
and *Endgame*, 56, 110
and Homer, 112
immobility, 114, 125
Job, The Book of, 110
Jones, Tom, 111
and Kafka, 111
landscape, 6, 111–12
language, 120
and *Malone Dies*, 125, 129, 132
Moran, 114–18, 119–22
mother, 109–13
mythical quality, 114, 118, 119
narration, 118–19, 122–4
parody, 134
picaresque novel, 103, 109, 111
and Plato, 113, 162
and Proust, 112
quest, 106, 109–14, 118–20, 125
religious overtones, 115–16
romantic sequences, 111, 112–13, 124